D1572408

ADVANCE PRAISE

Joshua Weiss, PhD., Co-Founder, Global Negotiation Institute and Senior Fellow, Harvard Law School Program on Negotiation

Lucia Kanter St. Amour has given us all a wonderful new book that demonstrates how effective negotiation is indeed a superpower. In fact, I would argue it is the mother of all superpowers! In a very readable manner, she helps the reader to grasp the nuances of negotiation through stories, anecdotes and popular exercises. When you finish the book, not only will you be a better negotiator, but you will have the foundation to continue on your own negotiation journey.

Thomas Wilmer, Award-winning NPR podcast producer and on-air host

Powerful. Moving. Provocative. Essential. A steady and stunning build to its exquisite climactic chapter, this book represents a long missing voice in the realm of negotiation—yet it defies genre. Lucia takes you by the hand, whispers secrets in your ear, hands you building blocks, and leads you deeper and deeper through a transformative journey. You may not emerge quite the same person as when you started - but you will definitely be a more resilient and radiant version of your former self.

Kwame Christian, Esq. M.A., Founder and CEO of American Negotiation Institute and host of the #1 negotiation podcast "Negotiate Anything"

Truly a Force for Good, Lucia has produced a critical missing link in the marketplace of negotiation literature. Inspiring and transformative, while certainly a work of skills building, it has a soul - and potential to generate not just better everyday negotiators, but more thoughtful participants in society at large. The time is overripe for more offerings like this that equalize the negotiating table, and make it fun and interesting in the process.

Alia Samad-Salameh, Principal, Global Labor Standards at Amazon

As a two decades labor negotiator - I'm loving this! Amazonians focus on super powers and the Super Tips provided are practical and useful in everyday life, which is often a series of negotiations. The usefulness of taking this out of the strict business setting or labor setting is wonderful. For women and other marginalized groups this is a great guidebook. Negotiation can be taught!

Colin Rule, Original eBay online dispute resolution system architect; President & CEO of mediate.com and arbitrate.com

I loved this book—couldn't put it down. It brings a complex topic right down to earth with funny and incisive stories. It's like chatting on the couch with your best friend, if your best friend happens to be a world-renowned expert in negotiation. This book is a treasure, and the world will be a better place if everyone reads it.

Florence Bienvenu, Attorney, Chief of Staff at United Nations Women, San Francisco

Once you hit chapter 15, there is truly no turning back. This is a work of careful and loving architecture, of fundamental skills, intellect, and storytelling. It's very moving. You wouldn't think a topic like this could be so moving. Lucia understands human complexity, and how to connect. She teaches all of us how to do it, too. It is a book to return to time and time again. Lucia, thank you for sharing this wonderful work, and for sharing so much of yourself!

Grande Lum, Obama Administration Director, Department of Justice's Community Relations Service; author of *The Negotiation Fieldbook and* **Co-Author of** *America's Peacemakers*
A fantastic book for anyone who wants to supercharge their negotiation powers. It is highly readable, thoughtful, personal, and full of useful ideas and tips to improve to your everyday negotiation skills. Lucia's energy, smarts, and passion for negotiation sparkled and inspired me throughout the entire book.

Mikkel Gudsoe, International Chamber of Commerce, Paris, competition judge and mediator; Danish fashion industry chief attorney and negotiator; professor of negotiation at Aarhus University
An amazing, refreshing and practical take on Negotiation...in fact... just human interaction! Very well written by an expert in her field with a strong handle on the pedagogy of influence, For the Forces of Good is easy to read with huge everyday take aways. This book should be read by everyone "new" as well as seasoned to negotiation!

Anita Christine Knowlton, Founding Director of the Center for Negotiation & Dispute Resolution at UC College of the Law, San Francisco
Captivating, layered, accessible, content-packed, and written in a warm, personal voice. There's nothing quite like it on the market in the way Lucia connects it all together. It's fantastic!

Janet Martinez, Director, Gould Center for Negotiation at Stanford Law School

*An engaging and all-gender synthesis of a skill that we all face daily: **negotiation**. Lucia's wonderful tone and writing style unpack negotiation as an essential function of everyday life. She matches our everyday demands with the power of equally everyday skills – if only we would be deliberate. She uses her deft storytelling power to synthesize a vast array of practical analysis and advice that the reader can leverage immediately. This book is a force for the reader's good.*

Mark D. Lucia, Director of Student Legal Services at University of California, Berkeley

The best kind of skill-building book: you'll learn a ton about handling negotiations big and small, even as you feel entertained and engaged by memorable and sticky anecdotes. It's a masterfully absorbing blend of storytelling, irresistible thought experiments, and practical tips that you can apply to your own life - from the moment you finish reading.

Lindsey Tran, Director, Global Employee Relations at Twitter

I was lucky enough to be one of Lucia's law students and have carried these lessons forward in my career. Learning to listen effectively and negotiate is a critical skill for everyone and should be a required competency for college students before they head into today's complex workplaces. This is a must read, especially for women and other marginalized groups who are often reluctant to negotiate. Lucia's storytelling is relatable, and entertaining. I especially love her balance of humor, vulnerability, and deep expertise which makes for such an engaging read.

Kim Harja, Director of Business Strategy, Employee Experience, Diversity and Inclusion at Charles Schwab

Like the banking, finance and technology sectors, negotiation is still perceived as reserved for a narrow cohort - an attitude that is as outdated as it is inequitable. This is the book that demystifies negotiation with great stories, skills, and a friendly, inclusive, expert voice. Absorbing and enriching, For the Forces of Good includes the everyday person and offers them agency. It levels the playing field without being a "For Dummies" book or compromising nuance and intellect. My only criticism is that it wasn't published sooner.

Veronica Bykin, Director of Engineering at Nike

As a woman in senior tech leadership roles, I negotiate on a regular basis, and had never felt comfortable doing it. This book gave me strength and confidence. Lucia's depth of expertise combined with a woman's voice & perspective, resonates and is very easy to relate to. Thank you so much for writing this book!!

Cassandra Bequary, Second Violin, Vancouver Symphony Orchestra

AMAZING. I can't emphasize enough how helpful, interesting - and I want to say vital - this piece is, with all the examples, tips, stories, and the layered approach. It starts out innocently enough: chocolates, planning, . . . and gradually while you aren't noticing, like a sublimely composed symphony, it builds until you are engrossed in a hypnotic experience. I devoured it and will read it again and again. Lucia is an absolute badass - brains and heart in the best proportions—and so generous in sharing her superpowers with the rest of us!

For the FORCES of GOOD

THE SUPERPOWER OF EVERYDAY NEGOTIATION

S. LUCIA KANTER ST. AMOUR

Copyright © 2022 Pactum Factum Press,
447 Sutter St, Ste 405, San Francisco, CA 94108

2022 Library of Congress Copyright Registration #: TXu002311527

Printed in the United States.

Cover and book design by Asya Blue Design.

ISBN 979-8-9864461-0-3 Hardcover
ISBN 979-8-9864461-1-0 Paperback
ISBN 979-8-9864461-2-7 Ebook

DEDICATION

For the two incandescent spirits, Julian and Nathanael, who were meant to alight with me as your flawed and passionate mother. I hope I have loved you enough and shown you enough how to love. For love is the nearest thing we have to a true superpower.

PREFACE

On a scorching summer day in 1981, when I was a ten-year-old girl in the small Illinois town (population four thousand) where I grew up, we had a garage sale. I decided to sell the play kitchen that I had outgrown and priced it at twenty dollars. On the weekend of the sale, my brother and I set up a lemonade stand where we refreshed bargain-hunters with Dixie cups of lemonade for twenty-five cents. A family came by with two young girls. I watched the girls' eyes light up when they spotted my play kitchen with cobalt blue sliding doors, bright yellow "fixtures," and cornflower blue and white plastic dishes. The father approached my parents and asked if the price was negotiable.

"You'll have to ask our daughter. The kitchen is hers," they said, gesturing to me at my lemonade table. The family walked toward me, and before the father could ask me about price, I preempted him with, "Would you like some lemonade?" He purchased four cups. That was one dollar I could knock off the price of my play kitchen, I calculated. He asked if I had any flexibility on price, and I replied, "What did you have in mind?" I glimpsed my own father out of the corner of my eye break into a smile. The father of the covetous girls offered me fifteen dollars, and I said OK. His girls were elated, and that made me feel pretty good.

Afterward, my parents praised me for my cunning negotiating skills. I had no idea what they were talking about. What had I done that was so special? I was just being myself and following my instincts. "Actually," my mother insisted, "what you did was pretty savvy."

Growing up in the 1970s and '80s in the Midwest, cruising on my trusty orange Schwinn bicycle tricked out with the glitter seat and fluttering ribbons I'd fixed to the handlebars, I pedaled freely in my well-worn Keds sneakers (*sans* helmet) to ballet and piano lessons, to Little League softball and the bookmobile. "Negotiation" was the sober and complicated undertaking of businessmen. It did not enter my mind. Had my fifty-year-old self traveled back to visit tween me, forecasting my fate as an attorney and an "expert" in negotiation who would lecture internationally on the subject, I would have thought that bionic future super-me sporting the chic suede knee-high boots was, in the vernacular of the day, "smoking dope."

In February 2022, when I launched my podcast, *Forces of Good: The Superpower of Everyday Negotiation*, I reminisced about the ten years that I taught negotiation at both University of California law schools at Berkeley and San Francisco* from 2003 to 2013, and a startling epiphany struck me: over the course of that decade, every single assigned text for my students was authored by . . . a man. It was all excellent content, certainly. I didn't assign my students any bilge. But where were the women, trans, nonbinary negotiation experts and authors? Certainly, it is not just men who have authored books and articles on negotiation and who teach the topic brilliantly. But the numbers pale in comparison to cisgender men.

---

* As of January 2023 University of California College of the Law, San Francisco is the new name for University of California Hastings College of the Law.

It was my dad, who had turned seventy-five in 2022, who suggested a harebrained idea: "You have so much content and experience. You are so passionate and competent about the subject. You should write a book."

Cue eye-roll. Oh please, Dad! That's just what the world needs. Another negotiation book. People don't even read anymore—they scroll social media posts. Besides, we already have too much "noise" in the blogosphere. I don't need to add to it.

I wonder if that's what other women said . . .

So here I am. As with my podcast, my goal is to help anyone become a better, more confident everyday negotiator. Because guess what? Turns out, negotiation is for everyone, everywhere, every day.

This book will cover a lot of ground, including nuts and bolts building blocks and exercises to strengthen your everyday negotiation muscles, and broader perspectives about human psychology, behavioral economics, brief historical perspectives, and social trends and their influence on your everyday negotiations. I'll discuss listening, planning, questioning, power and leverage, mental maps and traps, perspective-shifting, storytelling, imagination, choice theory, brain science, bullies, and free speech—we'll even talk about chocolate.

Well, now I've got your attention.

Think of this as your everyday superpower negotiation handbook. I will share many of the lessons and insights I've learned and taught in my twenty-five-plus years as an attorney and law professor teaching negotiation in the United States and abroad. But you don't need to be an attorney to negotiate. You don't need an MBA. You don't need to be a C-suite executive or a trained hostage negotiator negotiating life-or-death scenarios. I wasn't. I was that ten-year-old kid with a lemonade stand and a gently used pretend kitchen.

Negotiation is not much different from a muscle. The more you practice it, the more you exercise it, the stronger and more agile it develops as a natural everyday skill. Even superheroes undergo training and practice. Consider me your personal trainer and sidekick. If something doesn't resonate with you, you are free to reject it. But why not try it out first? You never know what might stick. Everyday negotiation is also an art; the inclusion of original art throughout the book isn't just fun eye candy, but a reminder of that ineffable aspect.

Finally, as asserted by the title, negotiation *is* a sort of superpower. The myth is that it's a superpower that you're either endowed with or you're not. The good news is that this couldn't be further from the truth: no need to be bitten by a radioactive spider in a research lab or spend your childhood on a remote and invisible island engaged in elite training. Negotiation is a superpower that anyone can harness—and to be used only for the Forces of Good.

S. Lucia Kanter St. Amour, *Garage Sale Lemonade.*
Watercolor and distressed ink on paper.

CONTENTS

CHAPTER 1

ARM-WRESTLING FOR CHOCOLATE: A NEGOTIATION APPETIZER

First question:

Who is the negotiator in your family, and how does that person do it?

In my family [spoiler alert] . . . it's me. But well before I was considered an expert in the field, certain personality characteristics contributed to effective negotiating in life—and that may very well be the case with you without you realizing it. For example, I truly like people. I'm genuinely curious about their life stories, where they've been, what their interests are, what makes them tick. The sincerity of that curiosity and my joy engaging with people is immediately discernible. In fact, if you listen to my podcast, *Forces of Good: The Superpower of Everyday Negotiation*, you can even hear it in my voice. Authentic curiosity about other people not only forms bonds but contributes to information gathering. I was also pretty good at truly listening and demonstrating that I had listened and asking additional questions. I've consciously studied and practiced a variety of additional skills over the years to expand my negotiation tool kit. By contrast, other people may be endowed with traits that didn't come naturally to me and vice versa: they had to learn and practice those that were comfortable for me from the start. So, I encourage you to think of that negotiator in your own family and what attributes make them so good at it. You don't need to be like them. You can be like *you* (we'll discuss this in a later chapter on negotiating style). But it's a useful thought exercise.

Negotiation is everywhere, every day. It happens in small, unsexy ways that may not be consciously perceived as negotiation. Whenever you want something from someone else, you negotiate. Generally, we can categorize negotiation into two types: (1) deal-making, and (2) dispute resolution. We negotiate a consumer complaint. We tacitly negotiate for the next open parking space at the grocery store; with our neighbors about fences, dogs, and noise; with colleagues and supervisors over assignments, compensation, vacation scheduling; even with ourselves (if I go for a run before work, I can relax and watch a movie after dinner). And who has kids? I rest my case . . .

The perception that negotiation skills are a specialized superpower to be left to "experts" but otherwise avoided whenever possible is, in a word, nonsense. Just because you aren't a trained Michelin star chef doesn't mean you can't prepare a perfectly satisfying spaghetti dinner for the family—in fact, I've preferred many home-cooked meals over celebrated posh restaurant fare in my life. Well before formally studying and teaching negotiation, when I was often in situations punching above my weight class, my preparation, listening, and observation skills alone made me a secret agent.

I'll let you in on a secret that may get me into trouble (as if that would be anything new): Negotiation "experts," especially those with consulting businesses, have a vested interest in promoting negotiation as some paranormal skill so that you think you need them ("Don't try this at home, kids!"). **Don't hire me.** Save your hard-earned money for a family vacation or a college fund for your kids and **do it yourself.** I can teach you!

So let's make you better and more confident at something that is an everyday experience—and that you may already be somewhat adept at doing, without knowing it.

We'll kick off this first lesson in everyday negotiation the same splashy way I initiated all my law students. I do wish to credit my mentor, Anita Christine Knowlton, the founding director of the Center for Negotiation and Dispute Resolution at UC College of the Law, San Francisco as the original designer of the curriculum we faculty members taught there.

It all started with chocolate and arm wrestling.

Yes, you read that correctly. Allow me to elaborate.

On the first class of the semester, I would pass out ten Hershey's Kisses to each pair of students, who were all seated at a U-shaped table in a seminar room. I instructed them that, for the purposes of this exercise, they should imagine that chocolate—and the attainment of it—was very important in their life. I would instruct the students to pair off with whoever was sitting next to them and to "assume arm-wrestling position" to determine how to divide up the chocolates between them. Then I'd say, "Go."

Admittedly, the typical responses included nervous laughter, blank stares, and incredulity. Invariably, we would have a student pairing including one individual of substantially greater physical prowess than the other. I would stand back and watch what unfolded. Note: I never actually commanded them to arm wrestle. I merely told them to "assume arm-wrestling position." After a couple of minutes, I'd announce, "STOP," usually much to their relief. That's when I would say "Let's debrief Round One."

Oh! That was just Round One? Hmm. What might Round Two look like, and what could transpire between the pairings of disparate size in which the student of more formidable body mass claimed all the chocolates?

Round One

How many just conceded to their partner? Why? When might that be appropriate?

How many didn't feel like wrestling and just split the chocolates—what happened there? Did they simply divide them evenly, five and five, or was there was a basis for division through discussion and discovery?

We discussed whether building a relationship mattered and being mindful of future negotiations. This was, after all, just the first class of a semester that would require many more simulations. We talked about just wanting to "win" or losing sight of the instructed goal—in this case to obtain chocolate; these were law students who were training to eventually represent clients whose goals may not agree with their personal preferences.

Round Two

For the second round, half the room was instructed to decide together how to divide the chocolates; for the other half of the room, I picked one student in the pairing to impose on their partner a division offer on a take-it-or-leave-it basis; no counteroffers allowed. Again, I announced, "Go!" followed by observation and another debrief (at which point they started to wonder how many more rounds and variations would ensue).

We talked about exchanging information to learn about each side's real interests—who did this? For instance, did one party have a greater need for the chocolates than the other due to depleted supplies, third parties relying on the commodity, etc.?

What did students think about having leverage (i.e., being the one in charge of imposing a division rule, which could have been an offer of only one chocolate to their partner and keeping nine for themselves) and not using it? If the leverage was used, who on the receiving end of the offer rejected it on principle because it was "unfair"? If so, did they lose sight of the goal? I had instructed them that the acquisition of chocolate was *very important*.

⟋ Everyday Super Tip

Just because you have leverage doesn't mean you use it (and doesn't mean you will hold on to it). Perhaps there's a longer game to be played or other factors more important than using leverage to "win."

This was ostensibly an example of distributive "fixed pie" negotiation (that is, limited/finite resources at stake), as compared with integrative "expanding the pie" negotiation (where more creative options and resources are explored beyond those transparent at the bargaining table). The chocolate exercises hinted that many times a situation that appears on its face to be purely *distributive* can be more *expansive* than originally thought.

Round Three

This time I introduced *asymmetry*: I told one student in each pairing they would lose two chocolates per minute that they didn't reach a deal, and the other student in the pairing would lose one chocolate per minute.

And again the debrief: We discussed other real-life examples of asymmetry. Perhaps one side has greater economic resources than the other: the luxury of time while their counterpart has a sense of urgency, greater access to information, more experience or expertise—even a greater sense of emotional vulnerability is a type of asymmetry.

The themes that emerged from the chocolate negotiations were basic:

- Reciprocity principle: if you make a gesture to someone else, the natural psychological response is for them to return in kind (or even disproportionately)
- Leverage versus power and the use or restraint of either attribute
- Cooperation versus competition
- Relationships

- Asymmetry
- Finite resources versus expanding options

Finally, I left them to ponder the hypothetical of *the Chocolate Baron vs. the Chocolate Pauper*. A chocolate pauper and chocolate baron are taking a walk in the woods when they come across a huge stash of chocolate. How might those players divide the chocolates between them and what might the considerations be in that negotiation? What does "fairness" mean? We discussed whether "fair" should be determined by objective data, subjective information, or some combination; whether historical factors should be considered (producing lively debates about the wealth gap, social justice, reparations, gerrymandering, and affirmative action); whether respective resources of each party should come into play; and when to bring in a third-party evaluator or decision maker to determine "fairness."

As burgeoning attorneys preparing to assume representation of clients with problems that mattered deeply to them, a difficult notion to accept (for attorneys and laypeople alike) is that "unfair" is not the same as illegal. This is a gray area where fine-tuned negotiation skills can play a game-changing role in everyday life.

⚡ Everyday Super Tip

Sometimes you need to walk away from a negotiation when no deal is better than a "bad deal." If you walk out on principle (e.g., "unfair"), take a beat to determine if you are also walking away from an offer on the table for something that you really need—despite aspects of "unfairness."

CHAPTER 2

PLAY NICE: RAPPORT AND HAGGLING

How do you feel about negotiating for a car purchase or a salary increase at work? Do you relish the experience? Do you put it off as long as possible, citing all sorts of excuses—*the timing isn't right, everything is fine how it is, why rock the boat*—and alphabetize your spices instead? We live in a culture—at least in the United States—where many people still consider negotiation cringey. When "No Haggle" car purchasing policies were introduced some years ago, they were warmly received by consumers who dreaded negotiating. Naturally these policies benefit the car dealerships over consumers, but they package it as a benefit to you to make you feel more "comfortable" about the car purchasing experience.

For many, negotiation is awkward and even synonymous with "conflict." Some even consider it tacky. Although I wasn't particularly afflicted with this shyness, I understand it. I savored a good haggle at the car dealership just as much as the thrill of the Scripps National Spelling Bee. In fact, if I learned that a friend or family member was in the market for a car, I'd giddily ask if I could tag along. Was that because I thought I would strike awe in a salesperson? Hilarious. I am hardly a remarkable presence. When I amble into a car dealership, heart rates don't quicken as salespeople mentally fortify their A-game to go toe-to-toe with the five-foot-two, 110-pound, plain-brown-haired and brown-eyed small-town midwesterner.

Indeed, when starting out as an attorney, I was routinely underestimated. This worked out splendidly for me. Everyday negotiation is a superpower, sure . . . but *invisibility* is also a pretty nifty superpower. I would accompany, say, a senior partner to a meeting with the Longshore union—and there I was at the bargaining table with my naive face and unimpressive physical stature. Other than an occasion on which one of them wondered aloud to the group, in reference to me, "Who invited the secretary of the Lollipop Guild?"—and was rewarded with chuckling all round—they dismissed me out of hand. While those guys (all men—just saying) forgot I was even in the room, *I was there.* As the comically large conference room chair swallowed me, I was listening (stick around for more juicy gossip on this point in chapter 5). To everything: not just what was being said but what was *not* being said and the spaces in between—the nonverbal glances and other cues—not to mention I had done my homework and was exceedingly well prepared.

Over time, I became less "invisible" and, I admit, I sort of missed it. By the way, Bob Bordone, a senior fellow at Harvard Law School and celebrated negotiation and mediation expert, offers specific advice on how to haggle for a car on his YouTube Channel. As with most negotiations, it involves a little advance planning (which we will turn to in the next chapter), and it's effective. I recommend his channel—aptly called *Bob Bordone*— for that and other short, practical, and entertaining videos on negotiating everyday situations, including the all-too-common family Thanks-giving quarrel (not that that's ever happened to you).

Perhaps some of the vexation we have with negotiation stems from an us-versus-them, win/lose, zero-sum paradigm. This is a game theory scenario in which one person's gain is equivalent to another's loss, so the net change in the wealth or benefit at stake is zero. A fundamental fear of rejection also tends to be a pervasive thought: "What if they say no?" Well, for one thing, most likely you are in no worse a position than before you asked. And here's an "aha!" tip reinforced by not just me but by Alexandra Carter in her book, *Ask for More*: Don't give up just yet. "No" isn't neces-sarily the end of the negotiation. Try responding to "No" with the question, "What are your concerns?" and you very well may find yourself continuing a new thread of the negotiation.

One very effective tool to overcome the "us-versus-them" appre-hension in negotiation is to build rapport with the other party. How do you do this, and why is it important?

Here's the *how*: Establish rapport with the other people engaged in the negotiation. This requires adopting a genuine attitude of curiosity about other people, and slowing down. If possible, take some time in advance to learn what you can about that person's background. Even if you know nothing about them, a simple, "How did you get involved in landscape architecture?" or "What brought you to this part of the country? Were you raised here?" or even the origin of their last name will do.

The key here is that your focus is on them and letting them know (without overtly saying it), "I see you as a human being." Then, pay attention to how they respond. Smile. Show an interest.

Demonstrate that you heard them with a recap: "Wow. Coming to California from the Midwest seems like it was quite a culture shock. And sounds like you don't miss the weather!" And then . . . notice if they reciprocate. Do they show an interest in you? It's OK if they don't, *and* the lack of reciprocation is also information to keep in mind.

Some quick do's and don'ts on rapport-building:

Do: Pay attention and listen (this is very different from waiting quietly for your turn to talk).

Don't: Bombard them with questions and cause them to feel they are being interrogated. This has the opposite effect of creating trust.

Do: Have a sense of humor.

Don't: Monopolize the conversation.

Do: Look for shared experiences to build upon, no matter how small or seemingly mundane.

Don't: Talk only about yourself.

Do: Make small talk! Although many people dread small talk or view it as superficial, it still creates connection; make small talk more meaningful by avoiding the same old "How are you? Good. How are you? Good" with a tiny dose or preparation: "How are you? Good—I just started this new [podcast/book/series about French cooking/hummingbirds/dog training, etc.] and am really enjoying it. Have you heard of it?"

Don't: Focus on the next question you want to ask.

Now for the *why* of establishing rapport: Genuinely connecting with another person satisfies a basic need for people to feel that they belong. In fact, people have a stronger need to belong than they do to be "right" factually (more on this point in chapter 11). When you demonstrate curiosity about someone else's life, attitudes, and interests, it is a validating and satisfying moment for them—not to mention it causes the brain to secrete dopamine because someone is paying attention to them. This is much better than the superficial dopamine "hit" through the "like" analytics supplied by social media.

Building rapport serves a couple of purposes: (1) it humanizes a negotiation and alleviates some of the defensive posturing, and (2) it provides a baseline of behavior for that person. That is, in a more/less relaxed state of mind while talking about a topic that is comfortable and easy for them, what is their tone of voice, volume, and vocal pacing? Do they tend to gesture a lot with their hands and body? Do they stop to pause and think? Do they smile? Baseline behaviors when an individual's defenses aren't triggered provide a basis for comparison later in the negotiation, when their words and actions deviate from the baseline.

You may not know the meaning of the deviation, but it's very important you don't make assumptions and commit the Othello error. This term was coined by renowned University of California, San Francisco psychologist Paul Ekman for his research in lie detection and emotional micro-expression. In the Shakespeare play *Othello*, Iago convinces Othello that Othello's wife, Desdemona, has been unfaithful to him with Cassio, a handsome soldier in Othello's army. Iago uses Desdemona's handkerchief, which she lost and he got his hands on, to help in his plan — he finds a way to slip it into Cassio's quarters. When Othello confronts his wife with the false accusation and evidence of the handkerchief, she becomes, understandably, fearful and behaves very nervously. Othello interprets her behavior as confirmation of her adultery and ultimately, he kills her. Only later does he discover that Iago planted the handkerchief and has been lying to him all along; the knowledge tragically undoes him. The lesson? Simply noticing a change from baseline may be enough to inform you it's time to pause and regroup—but not enough to take your preliminary assumptions as fact. You may even key into the correct emotions on display, but not know what it means.

As humans, we have a basic need to connect. We *think* we get that through screens, algorithms, and social media experiences. Although those moments and tools certainly offer some value and efficiency, they tend to be illusory. Minimal effort, knowledge, or preparation are required to advance that extra step to establish more genuine rapport—and you concede nothing by doing so.

Here's a **homework exercise** to get you practicing your everyday superpower (but don't worry—unlike my law students, I'm not grading you). It's a simple haggle you can do on Craigslist, with a NextDoor item for sale, or at the farmers market. As a first step, take a minute to build some basic rapport with the merchant/seller, even if just to make eye contact, flash a genuine smile, and ask how their day is going. If making an inquiry via email or text, you can accomplish this with some brief and friendly "small talk"—and emoticons are allowed! Show interest in the item with specific comments like, "I appreciate the craftsmanship of the wood inlay in this dining table. My grandfather used to work with wood." You can ask an open-ended, but strategically loaded, question, such as, "How flexible are you on price?" and then observe closely how they answer. At that point, you are well on your way!

⚡ Everyday Super Tip

If the haggle exercise seems too daunting, try this and then graduate to the haggle: The next time you're checking out at a store (assuming you still go to a brick-and-mortar store from time to time), ask simply (and smile!), "Do any other discounts or promotions apply to my purchase today?" If the answer is no, you're in no worse a position than when you started—you were going to buy the stuff anyway—and you certainly haven't lost any face. You may be surprised by how often the answer is "Yes."

Building rapport can be a daily practice without coupling it with negotiating. Once it's a habit and you combine it with a simple haggle exercise or more complex negotiation, it won't seem like an effort. Both rapport and the haggle exercise are also consistent with Robert Axelrod's *Evolution of Cooperation*. He explains basic behavioral economics and game theory that have been tested in iterated trials.

You may have interpreted the words in this chapter title, "play nice," as synonymous with "be nice." Certainly, you should be as nice as possible when negotiating! But the title is not meant to echo the Wendy Ward Charm School guide to "be nice" (complete with a "lilting voice—warm, gentle and animated" and instructions on how to sit in a chair such that the body formed an "S" shape). "Play nice" refers to a specific game theory model of behavioral economics and leverages smarts, sophistication and strategy—accomplished from an "S" position, an Amy Cuddy power pose, or criss-cross applesauce in yoga pants from the sofa while on a video conference. Axelrod taught four lessons to optimize cooperation and outcomes:

1. Be cooperative. Start off with a cooperative attitude, and expect your counterpart to do the same.

2. Be provokable. Be capable of retaliating if the other party stops cooperating.

3. Be retaliatory. If and when the other party stops cooperating, retaliate immediately and in kind.

4. Be forgiving. When the originally defecting party resumes cooperative behavior, so do you. Do not hold grudges. This is how groups realize more overall gains through cooperation. John Forbes Nash Jr., the Nobel laureate in economics, referred to it, casually, as the Most Beautiful Woman Theory, and it is featured in the bar scene of the film *A Beautiful Mind*, starring Russell Crowe.

⋀ Everyday Super Tip

Remember how you felt with your first real crush? Sure you do. Remember specific conversations with them? Probably not. People will remember how you made them feel more than your specific words and actions. (see chapter 4).

How Does Rapport Fit with Negotiations Using Technology?

Even before the dramatic shift to remote, asynchronous communications and interactions due to the COVID pandemic, everyday negotiations by email and online were the norm. Although negotiation through technology produces some unique issues, advantages, and disadvantages, the dynamics discussed throughout this book still apply, including establishing rapport.

Human-Machine Negotiation

The first factor to determine in any online negotiation is: Are you negotiating with a living human being or with software or artificial intelligence (AI)?

If you're involved in a consumer complaint or return with Amazon, eBay, or a similar online customer service representative, the "live chat" agent, at least to start off, is almost certainly AI. While the traditional rapport-building step may not seem to apply in that situation: (1) give it a chance because the algorithm may resolve your issue (quickly); and (2) it may not matter because the negotiation is purely transactional in nature so relationship isn't even a factor (more on this in the next chapter).

But don't be too quick to dismiss the idea of taking a cooperative, rapport-oriented approach with AI. You may be fascinated to learn that Axelrod's rules for cooperation among humans were gleaned through computer trials. In the 1980s, Axelrod conducted iterated trials of the basic game theory problem called Prisoner's Dilemma, in which the two players participated in a multi-round version of the game, neither player knowing when the game would end. The classic prisoner's dilemma is set up as follows: Two suspects, who we'll call Annie and Bennie, are arrested by the police. The police have insufficient evidence for a conviction and, having separated both prisoners, visit each of them and offer the same deal: if one testifies for the prosecution against the other and the other remains silent, the silent accomplice receives the full six-year sentence, and the betrayer goes free. If both stay silent, the police can only give both prisoners six months for a minor charge. If both betray each other, they receive a two-year sentence each. Each prisoner must make a choice—to betray the other or to remain silent. However, neither Annie nor Bennie knows for sure which choice the other will make. What will happen?

If reasoned from the perspective of the optimal outcome for the group (in this case, the two prisoners), the correct choice would be for both prisoners to cooperate with each other, as this would reduce the total jail time served by the group to one year total. Any other decision would be worse for the two prisoners considered together. When the prisoners betray each other, each prisoner achieves a worse outcome than if they had cooperated.

The Prisoner's Dilemma

	B stays silent (cooperates)	B betrays A (defects)
A stays silent (cooperates)	Both serve 6 months	A serves 6 years, B goes free
A betrays B (defects)	B serves 6 years, A goes free	Both serve 2 years

Axelrod hosted a tournament where participants submitted strategies to be used against all other competitors and a default competitor called "Random"—who would choose to defect/cooperate on a random level. Many well-known economists, game theorists, and computer scientists submitted strategies ranging from quite simple to extremely complex.

In the end, a basic program called *tit-for-tat* prevailed. The program simply began by cooperating and then proceeded by copying its competitor's last action (whether defection or cooperation). Here's the kicker: Axelrod then published the results and analysis of the tournament, allowed time for people to adjust their strategies to outthink tit-for-tat, and then hosted a second tournament . . . where tit-for-tat prevailed again! I often ask a prefatory question if routed to a live chat system. After the "agent" on the chat has introduced themselves with a chirpy greeting and a human-looking name, I type in the chat something to the effect of, "Are you a living human being or are you AI?" I still may not know for sure. An AI system, such as GPT-3, for example, is extremely sophisticated and can compose poetry, generate tweets, summarize emails, and answer trivia questions. But just because you are automatically led to AI for your negotiation doesn't mean (1) you are stuck there, or (2) it won't be effective and even swift.

AI might even negotiate better. It has crowdsourced millions of previous cases and aggregated data to "learn" behavioral pattern recognition and possible solutions that may not have occurred to you. While there are important ethical considerations to letting AI make our decisions for us, one thing we can give it credit for is helping to enable e-commerce by improving the dispute resolution process. Colin Rule, president and CEO of mediate.com and arbitrate.com, is widely recognized as one of the first architects of large-scale online dispute resolution (ODR) as the designer of the original consumer dispute resolution platform for eBay in 2003. At that time, he recalls that eBay was doing more transactions on a daily basis than the NASDAQ electronic stock market. In 99.9 percent of the transactions, people did what they're supposed to do: The buyer paid, the seller sent an item, and the buyer was satisfied. But that 0.1 percent of disputed items equated to about 60 million annual disputes, for which Rule designed an automated system with key words, prompts, and categories of questions to guide the buyer or seller through the process. Ninety percent of the 60 million annual disputes were resolved with technology alone.

"In all those cases, there [was] no human neutral," Rule told the Harvard Law publication *The Practice*. He elaborated: "A customer service rep [wouldn't] have to touch those cases. It was just the software that we built working with the parties to find resolutions. After all, we [had] 60 million disputes with only 25,000 employees worldwide. If all we ever did was work at disputes with our 25,000 people, we wouldn't even get through a third of that in a year."

S. Lucia Kanter St. Amour, *Tit-for-Tat Robot*. Watercolor on paper.

Human-Human Negotiation

Now let's assume someone with a pulse is your negotiation counterpart online or via email. Many people receive and send hundreds of messages each day, and at a speed that often compromises thoughtful word choice, skipping the extra sentence or two that could have made the difference in connecting with the recipient. Video conferencing adds the synchronous and visual aspects of communication but still doesn't capture the nuances of being in the same room with other living and breathing human beings. In a brick-and-mortar setting, we also know for certain who is present and who is absent, whereas video and voice conferencing allow for the possibility of eavesdroppers or others on the other side of the call coaching your counterpart. The "protection" provided by the screen can also lead to more insensitive language, threats, and bluffs as compared to the in-person experience. Then there's screen fatigue to take into account.

Despite these hiccups, if you can negotiate in synchronous time— that is, all together, whether in person, by voice call, or by video call—it is generally more gratifying than asynchronous deal-making or conflict resolution. As advised by Victoria Medvec in her book *Negotiate without Fear*, "Say it, don't send it." By communicating an issue, question, or offer in synchronous time, you can immediately evaluate the reaction and calculate how you may need to adjust.

Recognizing the reality that asynchronous communication will most likely play some part in your negotiation (though, again, try not to rely on it exclusively if you don't have to), here are a few tips for negotiating asynchronously while availing yourself of the tried-and-true lessons in this book:

- Just because the forum is electronic, don't brush aside the rapport-building step. Not only does it serve as an ice-breaker, but it also nurtures human relationships. Relationships are how deals are made, and relationships require attention.

- Have an agenda for that particular call or message. A technology-based negotiation will likely need to be broken down into several sessions.

- As for email: No matter how eloquently written, a lengthy email that outlines all of your requests and justifications in a single communication is (a) not strategic (showing all your cards at once) and (b) unlikely to be appreciated—or even read in its entirety.

- As with setting an agenda, emails should be tailored to just one or two points and kept brief—but not too brief (an email that says, "As discussed, see attached" and attaching six documents for the reader to review and figure out how it all connects is not very helpful). I often include a mini "table of contents" in an email of even just two brief paragraphs. In fact, this is one of the tools that led to the publication of this book. As a debut author, I researched agents that fit the genre and reviewed their submission guidelines. Most required a simple email query with a brief summary of the project before deciding to invite any content. They also warned of a four- to six-week lag time for an expected response. I decided to query four agents while the manuscript was undergoing review by a trusted editor, not expecting a reply for some time. After my salutation and initial introduction, my brief two-paragraph email was prefaced with:

In this email:

1. *What is my book about?*
2. *Why should it be published (and become a best seller)?*
3. *Why am I the best person to have written it?*

Three of the four agents replied within twenty-four hours, requesting a formal submission.

◢ Everyday Super Tip

Make it easy for them! The easier you make the job of digesting your message for your audience, the more likely you are to garner agreement.

- On a video call, be aware of your background. Everything around you communicates something about you. Try to establish eye contact. This is better accomplished by turning off the feature that allows you to view yourself, and looking into your computer's camera rather than the other person's face on the screen.
- Prepare for an online, email, or video negotiation, and treat it just like you would an in-person negotiation. Do not multitask (checking emails or social media alerts while the other person is speaking). Genuinely engage with the other people in the virtual room, and give them (and the agenda) your full attention. Silence any other device that could make a pinging noise. *You* will get more out of it yourself and even *feel* better about the time.

- Summarize points in a follow-up email, and secure agreement that you have understood correctly.

- Find ways to be encouraging, make small talk, and keep the rapport going throughout the call or email. This may be the third Zoom call for your counterpart that day, or their ninetieth email exchange. Use the language of empathy in your communications (which we will discuss in a later chapter). Be thoughtful with your word choice, the use of ALL CAPS, and exclamation points!!!! Your talking head and/or written words, unlike the communication of your full body in-person, is all someone has to infer your messaging.

Recognize that where a negative inference *can* be made, it *will* be made (more on this point in chapter 11). So remember: Play Nice!

CHAPTER 3

"LITTLE OLD LADIES": NEGOTIATION PLANNING, POWER, AND LEVERAGE

For the ten years I taught negotiation at UC College of the Law, San Francisco, I assigned my students the task of submitting a planning memo before each simulated negotiation exercise. I will level with you: they considered it tedious "busy work," to which I would say, and still do, "You're welcome."

Entering into a negotiation without preparation or a plan is like walking into a casino with an open wallet. Even when I could discern from the contents of my students' memos that they approached it as a perfunctory "check the box" exercise, I didn't particularly care. They were still developing an important habit. Generally, I recommended that they use the planning guide that G. Richard Shell offers in Appendix B of his book *Bargaining for Advantage*, which was also an assigned text and an excellent primer on negotiation, which includes some great anecdotes. This chapter will discuss some aspects of that guide, supplemented by other sources and my own notes from experience over the years. I've organized it into ten dance moves. But just reading these steps, without doing more, isn't enough. It's no different from sitting on the sofa while watching the workout video. You need to actually perform the moves to reap the results. Hunker down and flesh out each step, in writing—even for just twenty minutes. That's how you will build the "muscle memory" required for planning to evolve from the gawky middle school dance to the dynamic hip hop feat of artful athleticism.

Step 1: Consider the Context, Players, and Problem Statement/Issue Identification

Consider the context of this negotiation. Is it "high stakes" (a subjective notion that only you can define. See chapter 18)? Richard Shell organizes negotiation into four basic categories: Relationship, Transactional, Balanced Concerns (a hybrid of the first two categories), and Tacit Coordination (examples of which would be drivers at a four-way stop sign determining who goes first, or not eating the last cookie so you don't get in trouble with your spouse). So, is preserving the relationship important? Is the context purely transactional? Is it a blend of transactional and relationship?

Which conflict "mode" would be most effective for the context (more on modes in chapter 12). This first step should also include an effort to define the problem(s)/issue(s) at stake and create an agenda for the negotiation. It's easy to lose track of issues once you're in the thick of bargaining. Think about comparing your problem statement with the other party in advance and setting an agenda of the issues all parties wish to cover (see final chapter for an example). This can save time at the outset of bargaining, manage expectations, and minimize frustrations from cropping up right out of the gate. At least you'll be on the same page to start.

Find out who will be participating in the negotiation, and perform some internet sleuthing. Where are they from? What is their background and education? What makes them tick? Do you both like dogs? What other commonalities or potential obstacles can you discover? This step will help build rapport, as discussed in chapter 2. Also think about who YOU need with you to (a) strategize and (b) attend the negotiation. You don't need to go it alone!

⚡ Everyday Super Tip

Recognize when you need help, *and ask for it.* Generally speaking, people want to be helpful. Even superheroes need help (think Avengers)!

Step 2: Define Interests

People often come to the bargaining table expressing positions. What the celebrated negotiation scholars and authors Roger Fisher and William Ury have preached for years is the importance of moving past the stated positions to the underlying interests: that is, piercing the WHAT to get to WHY something is important to them. Consider different types of interests: concrete (such as financial), psychological (such as a feeling of safety), and procedural (such as timing). And consider whether they may be shared or conflicting interests with the other side. Actually make a chart like this—and we'll pretend it's for a used car purchase.

My Interests	Their Interests (known or guesses)
Reliable transportation	Quick sale?
Fits my budget	Get the highest price they can
"Cool" factor	Goes to a "good home"?
Fuel efficient	Offload gas-guzzler and commit to all-electric vehicles

Step 3: Set Specific Goals and Know Your Reservation Point
Too many people approach a negotiation without any goals at all, or a goal of "doing the best I can." That's not a goal.

Let's consider the example of Girl Scout Cookies. Each spring, all around the United States, the Girl Scouts ply Americans with their famous cookie sales. When I participated in Girl Scouts of America in the early 1980s, I actually went door to door in my neighborhood with my sales sheet and my pitch. When the cookies arrived for me to distribute, I loaded them up in my red Radio Flyer wagon—I'm not making this up—and pulled the wagon around the neighborhood, for miles, delivering the cookies. My goal was to sell 100 boxes, and I was ecstatic when my own mom purchased ten. That's not how it works anymore. Girl Scouts—with their parents at their side—set up tables outside commuter train stations and grocery stores. Parents email friends asking them to buy cookies for their Scout. Some troops set up a form email for the individual Scouts to send under their own name and allow for cookie orders directly through the troop website.

What is the purpose of the Girl Scouts of America cookie campaign (other than to addict consumers to Thin Mints and Samoas)? According to the Girl Scouts of America website, it's fivefold: to learn about (1) goal setting, (2) decision making, (3) money management, (4) people skills (see rapport in chapter 2), and (5) business ethics. From 2009 to 2019, I conducted my own little experiment each cookie-selling season, in addition to subjecting my three nieces to this line of questioning during the time they participated in Girl Scouts. I would approach a table outside a grocery store, smile brightly, and say, "Hi! How exciting! It's Girl Scout Cookie season!" to which I'd be met with, "Would you like to buy some cookies?"

I'd say, "Quite possibly. I'd like to chat with you a little first. Do you mind if I ask a few questions?" (See chapter 10) While I generally received consent, their smile would already devolve into a frozen grimace. I would keep smiling and reassure them it was perfectly OK to not know the answers to my questions, how I had been part of Girl Scouts when I was young, and how supportive I was of their endeavor. Then I'd ask if they knew what the purpose of the cookie-selling enterprise was (how many of the five objectives could they recite?); their troop goal; their individual goal; how their troop intended to use the proceeds; and then, "This last question is tricky, and I don't expect you to know the answer. But I'm just so curious . . . do you happen to know how much of the cookie profits your troop keeps compared to Girl Scouts of America Corporate?"

Mind you, I asked the questions one at a time, not in rapid succession (I'm annoying and pedantic but not a monster). In ten years of this experiment—often to the chagrin of one or both of my sons, who had accompanied me to the store—a couple of dominant behaviors prevailed. The parents would almost invariably start to answer for the Scout; I'd flash my smile in their direction and request as cheerfully as I could, "I'd love to hear directly from your Scout if that's OK?" (which was typically met with pursed lips and a furrowed brow by said parent). And, the Scouts could answer an average of only one of the questions. For the most part, they had no idea about goals and had not wondered about purpose. This is an example of blindly entering into an enterprise—for tradition? For the authoritative organization or local tribe? Simply because people love cookies, and that's reason enough?—and not thinking about a plan, information gathering, or goal setting.

Nonexistent, vague, and unprincipled goals lead to lackluster results. Richard Shell teaches us that negotiators who develop high, specific, justifiable goals accomplish approximately 40 percent better outcomes than negotiators with amorphous goals. Let's break this down:

High means a starting point that you can communicate with a straight face, though not one that you realistically expect to achieve. Leave yourself room to make concessions and show the other side that you have come their direction. People like to feel that the outcome of a negotiation was "hard won." So, counteroffers do serve an important purpose in the negotiation dance.

Specific means crunching numbers for a precise calculation, as well as any other attributes needed to make your goal durable and practical (who, what, when, where, how).

Justifiable means that when you are asked how you arrived at that demand, you can refer to objective standards and metrics to back it up. This works both ways: When the other side presents their offer, you should always ask, "How did you arrive at that?"

Now imagine the confidence and motivation cookie-selling Girl Scouts might enjoy equipped with information, specific goals, and a sense of purpose. Imagine how it could help them build rapport, focus on specific goals, and affect both the experience (more fulfilling) and outcome (sell even more cookies).

You also need to know what your **Reservation Point** (aka "Bottom Line") is—that is, the point at which you walk away from the bargaining table because no deal is better than a "bad" deal. This includes what Fisher and Ury call an analysis of BATNA: understanding what your—and the other side's—Best Alternative to a Negotiated Agreement is (that is, if you can't get a deal, what's your and their best backup plan?). You should also consider your and their WATNA (Worst Alternative) and MLATNA (Most Likely Alternative).

Using the example of searching for a specific, hard-to-find model used car which you've been looking for for six months before finding one for sale that is exactly what you want but is out of your price range:

- BATNA: Find a similar make/model that is more readily available; find some nonmonetary value I can offer the seller for this car, such as my master mechanic services in the future.

- WATNA: Remain inflexible about the make/model and keep taking the bus, which is consistently late, makes me late for work, and causes stress for my family and me.
- MLATNA: Take on some side work or ask my brother for a loan to raise extra money to bridge the difference between the top of my budget and the lowest I think the seller will go on price.

Step 4: Determine Applicable Standards & Norms
Objective or authoritative standards and norms are those that neither party can manipulate. Why should you look to these?

- Makes the negotiation principled.
- Helps you defend a position.
- Helps you avoid appearing weak or arbitrary.
- Builds trust because you are referencing external standards.

Some common examples include replacement cost, competitor's price, community practice, scientific merit, depreciated book value, precedent, and what a judge or jury would decide. Be specific about standards or objective criteria that will favor you, standards you believe they will use, and standards or status quo you think need to be challenged, and think about how to work with the other side's standards or convince them that yours are more relevant or appropriate:

Mine	Theirs	My Counterarguments
Bluebook value	"Classic Car" value	Having a sentimental attachment to a car doesn't mean it's "classic" (but show empathy)
Ongoing cost of maintenance now that warranty is expired	Reputation and past record of this make/model for reliability and "low maintenance"	Conduct my own research on online auto discussion groups about maintenance cost of this make/model
Gasoline cars are losing value due to climate change and shift to electric, which should factor into price.	Gasoline cars will become scarcer and difficult to find, which should factor into price.	Appeal to environmental responsibility

Step 5: Evaluate Leverage

Assess who you think has more leverage going into the negotiation. Let's dive a little deeper on this point.

Power and leverage are not synonymous but are often articulated interchangeably. Who has more power in the negotiation? Who has leverage? How can that leverage be influenced?

Well, what's the difference?

Power is the strength, ability, or resources to do something or act in a particular way (subtext—a way that can also control other people or outcomes).

Leverage is having something that someone else wants or needs and thus the ability to influence power (subtext—to affect other people or outcomes).

Hmm. Still a little obtuse? Let's look at a couple of concrete examples:

- Consider the massive real estate developer who has successfully purchased all but one tiny home in the area designated for a new medical research campus. That home is owned by an eighty-year-old woman (in good health, so she's presumably not going anywhere) whose grandfather built the house, was raised there, and raised her own family there. She has communicated to the developer that there is no price they can put on that house. It's simply not for sale. She's just a "little old lady," and they are the big powerful developer. But she's got the leverage.

- Many of us are parents. Kids are great natural negotiators: they are relentless about what they want, highly motivated to get it, unconcerned about you saying no, persistent, and imaginative. Between a parent and a three-year-old child, the parent is the more powerful party. We are bigger and stronger and have a more developed brain, more experience, and better command of our fine and gross motor skills to accomplish tasks. But if you want your child to eat their peas, the child has the leverage. Sure, you can use threats and bribes. I'm not going to pretend that figurative carrots and sticks aren't useful implements in the parental toolbox. But ultimately, you cannot force the child to eat the peas. Only they can do so. They've got you in the crosshairs, and how you respond is really a test of your own temperament, behavior, and strategy. Not only might your ego be on the line ("I can't let them win this one. I need to maintain who's in charge"), but shaping future behaviors might be on your mind ("If I surrender on the peas, what am I signaling? I lose credibility and they'll learn that they don't have to listen to me in the future"). Leverage is nuanced and can be a real thorn in the side of the more "powerful" party at the negotiating table when they don't have it.

Now for the punch line: leverage can shift. The party who starts with it doesn't necessarily hold on to it. Perhaps there's a way for the real estate developer to affect conditions to change the situation (e.g., start the demolition on the properties surrounding our "little old lady," creating conditions so intolerable that she finally caves). Perhaps you can use a third party as an influencer: that favorite uncle whom your child constantly imitates happens to be visiting for dinner and delightfully devours their peas, exclaiming how good and healthy and strong peas make them feel . . . causing your child to gobble down their peas so they can be just like Uncle Mark. Or maybe ask yourself what makes it so important to *you* that your child eat the peas? *Can* you let it go? Can you substitute something else for the peas that would satisfy the interest at stake and you can both get on with life?

This brings us to a secret of negotiating that's hiding in plain sight. After the planning is complete, and you are actively negotiating, remain nimble. Often new information is presented through the course of the negotiation. Pay attention. Have you learned something that impacts your BATNA or that enables you to influence the other side's BATNA? You may need to take a break to develop additional options or conduct more research. You may need to adjust your expectations or your bottom line accordingly. Assimilating (after validating it) that new information and assessing how it affects your options (and possibly shifts leverage) is one of the unsung superpowers of great negotiators—especially these days when it seems people's opinions are expressed as incontrovertible fact and they are just the opposite of open-minded or flexible about new or different information (more on this topic later).

The point is, leverage is dynamic and can be a shell game in negotiation—so keep your eye on that moving ball. For an entertaining depiction of shifting leverage, watch the 2003 film *Pirates of the Caribbean: The Curse of the Black Pearl.*

⋰ Everyday Super Tip

Avoid the rookie mistake of underestimating *anyone*—especially little old ladies. They've lived a long life, they've seen things, they've had experiences you haven't, and they know things. Respect to little old ladies everywhere!

Step 6: Consider Invisible Influencers—Third Parties
Do you need to consider the impact of a deal on any third parties?
Can a third party be used as an audience/excuse/justification (e.g., shareholders; parent organization of a school; union members;

the diversity and inclusion committee of your company; or even general notions of reputation in the community)? Don't make the mistake of omitting necessary decision-makers from the bargaining table, however. One of the basic requirements for each party in a mediation with me is that any necessary decision-makers must be present. If you've been negotiating over the course of hours, days, or weeks without the participation of a final decision-maker, the precious but delicate house of cards you've built can tumble. If they haven't been one of the architects, you run a high risk that they just won't get it, and it's too easy for them to reject a lot of hard work. They haven't had any skin in the game or taken the time to be a part of the whole story arc.

Step 7: Find a Big Paper Clip— Imagine Possible Creative Ideas/Proposals

Although true brainstorming is time-consuming and best accomplished together with the other parties, it's worthwhile to start this in the planning stage. How can you build on shared interests, bridge conflicting interests, create options? Be creative at this stage without "culling" your ideas too much. The culling comes later when you gauge if the other side is open to the idea, and then you start to test the practicality of creative options. While creativity is a wonderful attribute, it must be combined with durability.

We dedicated an entire class session at the law schools just to brainstorming. I'd stand in front of the class with a large butterfly-shaped paper clip. I'd say, "This class is forming a corporation, and this is our invention. What are all its possible uses?" Then I told them we couldn't stop until I ran out of room on the chalkboard (yes, I used a chalkboard—and an overhead projector. Aren't you now totally impressed that I'm keeping up with modern times and hosting a podcast?). This process usually started slowly, but I would literally stand in silence waiting for them to yell out ideas: an earring, drain cleaner, Q-tip, retainer, nose picker, car hood ornament, pet tag, cherry pitter . . . and at some point, when the ideas were running low, I'd prompt them with, "What if we had 100 of them? A hundred thousand of them joined together? What if we melted it down?" and we'd be off and running again with much bigger ideas for power turbines, fences, and machinery of social protest and change. Then we would develop goals and interests for our corporation (e.g., legally compliant, environmentally responsible, cost efficient, readily available or even open-source, compliant with safety standards, etc.) and start to cross off the ideas that didn't match.

⚡ Everyday Super Tip

In the planning stage of negotiation, feel free to let your hair down and get a little "crazy" because you never know when a seemingly wild idea, while not practical itself, could *lead* to a really brilliant and practical one.

Step 8: Plan for Use of Information

Do not skip over this step! Richard Shell suggests a "Give/Get/Guard" chart, which means considering what information you are willing to give (or want to make certain they hear), what information you need to try to get from the other side, and what information you need to guard from the other side discovering. Let's break this down:

Give. What information will you give them and how (and with what timing)? What's the purpose of *giving* information in a negotiation? I mean, don't you just want to *get* information from the other side? Well, giving helps the relationship, it provides a starting point (and there may be reasons that you want to be the person to establish that starting point), it can trigger reciprocity, it signals leverage, and it helps you offer and justify concessions later on.

Get. What do you need to learn from the other side? The purpose of *get* is, again, assessing leverage, discovering true interests so that you might satisfy them, discovering obstacles, assessing credibility, testing assumptions, and evaluating the standards they are using. It also helps you reevaluate if necessary (and it's often necessary).

Guard. This is the information you don't want them to have and why. You may need to guard it in the face of persistent questioning. How can you do that? You can:

- Provide a partial answer.
- Provide a limited/qualified answer (e.g., "I can't make such an offer at this time").
- Answer a different question.
- Misconstrue the question.
- Ignore the question.
- Answer a question with your own question.
- Bluff.
- Be transparent ("I can't share that with you").
- Negotiate information for information, or . . . my personal favorite . . .

SILENCE. You've heard how nature abhors a vacuum? Apply this law of physics to the other party. Seriously, if you can get comfortable with twenty seconds of silence in the face of questioning, start mentally counting backwards from twenty and by the time you hit twelve, watch how they will fill that silence themselves with more talking.

Give	Get	Guard
My appreciation of this make/model car	Why are they selling it?	The fact that this may be considered a classic
Information on my research of similar cars and sales prices to set desirable purchase range	Idea of "irrational" valuation of the car such as sentimental value or idea that it is definitely a "classic"	That I already have this make/model and am purchasing to scavenge for the passenger door to replace mine, which is a part impossible to find
I am a master mechanic and know what I'm talking about	Any prior accidents or body repair	Once I replace my door, I will likely sell off the remainder of this car for parts

Step 9: Calculate a Concession Plan

Related to Step 3, map out the concessions you are willing to make during the course of bargaining. Think through all the possible ways you can build concessions into the negotiation to show the other side you are "giving up" something(s). Though

I stand by my advice in chapter 2 to "make it easy" for the other side to engage, I've also advised how people like to feel that the outcome of the negotiation was "hard won." On the surface, those two conditions may seem at odds with each other, but they demonstrate how people are multitudes, and a negotiator who understands human complexity is well served. Concessions can be monetary or otherwise; they can be tangible or intangible. Smart negotiators even plan for "false concessions," that is, the appearance of giving up something that does not, in reality, matter much to you. When a Hollywood agent was asked about his negotiation strategy, he advised, "Always leave a bagel on the table." The point is to increase the other side's satisfaction with the deal.

Step 10: Reflect Personally
Think about ideas for increasing your effectiveness and managing your own emotions, reactions, and personal goals in this particular negotiation. Take a few moments to consider what could trigger you emotionally and strategies for regulating yourself if that happens (more on this in chapter 12). Do you need help? If so, get it. If you are negotiating in a team or with your attorney, is there a code word—or secret baseball hand signals—that you craft in advance that lets the other person know it's time for a break?

Note that this requires true presence of mind in the negotiation. When I was a fledgling attorney, I would hold a small smooth stone in my hand; it was cool to the touch and helped me remain calm and grounded. Did I still get overwhelmed or feel out of my depth? Yes. But the key was that I didn't yield to false pressure tactics and knew enough to adjourn and reconvene after I'd had time to think or consult a more senior colleague for advice.

⚡ Everyday Super Tip

If the other side is applying pressure for an immediate response, this is a flag. How likely is it that pressure is "real" versus manufactured by them? In fact, you've probably just gained valuable information: that *they* are in a rush. Absent a deadline by an authoritative and objective source, don't be hurried. If it's a power play on their part, making them wait can shift the power. Ditto for feeling confused: chances are it's *because something is confusing* (and they may be trying to make it so), not that you are a dummy.

There's a scene in the movie *Butch Cassidy and the Sundance Kid*, starring Robert Redford and Paul Newman, that I used in my law class. Butch and Sundance are the two leaders of the Hole-in-the-Wall Gang. Butch is all ideas; Sundance is all action and skill. Well, they robbed one too many trains, and a highly specialized posse starts tracking them wherever they go.

In this scene, the posse is closing in on them and they've literally run out of land. They have arrived at a high cliff over a raging river, and the posse is gaining on them with each passing second. They are cornered and arguing over what to do. I would watch the scene with my law students, and I would pause it just before the characters make their decision. I would ask the students to analyze it as a negotiation. What would the negotiated agreement entail?

Surrendering to the posse—it's probably the best way to remain alive and possibly negotiate some . . . I don't know . . . plea bargain? Did they do that in the Wild West? Absent that, what's their BATNA? To jump from the cliff down to the river and hope to survive the fall. What's their WATNA? Death. What's their MLATNA? Well, death again—either from the fall or by drowning or at the hands of the posse. Oh, and one of them finally admits he can't swim. And then I'd hit play to reveal what happens next . . .

Julian Kanter, *What Plan?* Acrylic on canvas.

CHAPTER 4

"SPIDEY SENSE" IN NEGOTIATION: PLANNING MEETS INTEROCEPTION

Are you the sort of person who makes a list before going to the grocery store and sticks to the items on the list while in the store? Do you skip the list altogether, grab some produce and staples like milk and eggs, and then browse the frozen and prepared foods sections for weekly dinner ideas? If you're anything like me, you do both: plan something of a menu for the week and list ingredients for those recipes but stay open to something that inspires you as you wind the shopping cart from aisle to aisle (*Ooh. Pomegranate seeds would be fun in our salads this week*). This strikes me as a winning combination of planning and flexibility, which translates well to other facets of life: travel, parenting, group projects. It's no different in negotiation.

I emphasized the importance of planning in some detail in the last chapter. It's common to become emotional, confused, or simply tired during the negotiating story arc. Having that plan to anchor and refocus you is key. And it's that anchor that provides you the freedom and comfort to be flexible and trust your instincts in the moment. Look, it's easy to infer a mixed message. These days, we are bombarded by catchy, pseudo-psychology marketing phrases that tell us to have a growth mindset . . . lean in . . . do something that scares you every day . . . get out of your comfort zone . . . and some people interpret this type of advice as meaning you can skip the stodgy planning and "just go with your gut."

But it's the planning stage that actually allows you to pay attention to your "gut" instincts in the negotiation and feel confident about them.

What I'm really talking about is *interoception*, which is defined as the sense of the state of the body—both conscious and unconscious. You might even call it your "Spidey Sense." Interoception encompasses visceral signaling projected to the brain via neuropathways and typically manifests in the cardiovascular, respiratory, and gastrointestinal systems. In 2021 the *New York Times* journalist Ezra Klein took a deep dive into this subject in an interview with science writer Annie Murphy Paul about her book, *The Extended Mind*.

In the interview, Klein and Paul discuss the problem with the long-standing and all too dominant analogy of our brain as a computer—that we have taken this ill-suited metaphor of the mind and built social infrastructure with it in the way of schools, workplaces, and productivity models that don't fit how a living organism operates. That is what the brain is: a living organism that has evolved over time in many contexts—and mostly outdoors—and must be understood on its own terms. Cognitive processing is just part of the information our brains supply us, while much more "thinking" is emanating from within the body and unconsciously. Studies of Wall Street traders identified those who seem to make more money when they're more interoceptively attuned, that is, better at reading their own body signals. When our nervous system is aroused, it's feeding us information. Ignoring these sensations as simply "fear" or "anxiety" or inconsistent with "leaning in" or a "growth mindset" is no different from dismissing evidence consciously driven by the executive functioning of the brain.

⚡ Everyday Super Tip

Don't dismiss the information your body is communicating. I have long cautioned against hailing rational analysis as the best or only method of making decisions or engaging with others—in negotiation, in conflict, or in the vagaries of everyday interactions. Those who can harness the powers of the mind and the body and reference them at appropriate moments—well, they are next-level everyday negotiating superstars. And that can be you!

If you know you've prepared well for a negotiation, despite all the multilayered dynamics tumbling toward you during that negotiation, trust the confidence of your preparation and listen to your interoception. At the very least, hit the pause button to allow yourself time to reflect. In very few circumstances do you need to be rushed into a decision. Urgency is commonly manufactured as a pressure tactic. If your body is feeling a sense of stress due to urgency, test the urgency and whether it is a valid factor in the negotiation. How many times have you been casually browsing for an item online and you come upon a website where, coincidentally, everything is 20 percent off until the end of . . . that day! Oh, how lucky you happened across this website at this serendipitous moment! You had just been casually looking, but now you'd better go ahead and complete the purchase before that deal ends! You have likely been drawn into a classic sales ploy and use of a cognitive trap called the *scarcity effect* (creating scarcity of time—"Act now! This offer won't last!" More on mental maps and traps in chapter 13). Well, maybe and maybe not. If that coupon vanishes tomorrow, another will probably appear soon enough.

I can personally vouch for the interoception experience in negotiation. In my career, I've done I don't know how many negotiations and mediations, and thousands of depositions (this is the particularly harrowing mechanism during the discovery process of litigation where a witness is subjected to unforgiving questioning under oath, with their testimony recorded by a certified court reporter. It is not for the faint of heart and should not be undertaken without the assistance of legal counsel). For many years, for every deposition I kept a log of the attorney on the other side: their name, the date, and a little dossier detailing their overall personality, their level of preparation, their questioning style—clear and organized, or confusing and compound? If the latter, did it seem intentional to disorient the witness or like just a lack of skill? Did they "play nice" with the witness? (Being deposed is not fun!) To the court reporter? To the interpreter? Did they try to sneak in prohibited questions to test me and whether I was paying attention? (I was!) Did they make small talk? What was going on in their life? Not only did this make them feel good because I was treating them like a human being, but it also benefited my own client that I had built rapport with them. The fact that I kept a log did not mean my curiosity about their lives and my bonding wasn't genuine. It very much was!

✔ Everyday Super Tip

Rapport, rapport, rapport! It never goes out of style. It was no coincidence that I achieved a high settlement rate for clients right then and there on the day of their deposition.

Why am I telling you about this dossier, and what does it have to do with interoception? I had over a thousand names in that log. I certainly didn't remember everyone over all the years with my conscious mind. Before any deposition, I'd look at what opposing attorney's name appeared on the Notice of Deposition and, even if I didn't consciously recognize the name . . . my *body* would react. I'd feel maybe a sense of contentment wash over me and not know exactly why. Or, I'd feel a pit forming in my stomach and wonder, "Hmm. What's that about?" Then I'd open my log and look up the name, read the notes on that person, and think, "Ah! That explains the feeling of dread. It's not going to be an easy day." *My body remembered.* This was before I even had heard the word *interoception* and it fascinated me.

✔ Everyday Super Tip

I actually thought I was special to experience these sensations . . . like endowed with extrasensory gifts. Maybe I am, but then so are you. I know now that anyone can tap into the information their own body is sending them.

I'll close out this chapter with a bedtime story. Show of hands how many of you have read—and/or read to your children—Margaret Wise Brown's famous children's book, *Goodnight Moon*?

I thought so.

Turns out, Margaret Wise Brown was way ahead of her time in understanding interoception. *Goodnight Moon* did not first appear on a public library shelf until 1972—twenty-five years after it was first published. Why? Anna Holmes contributed a detailed portrait of Brown's life in *The New Yorker*, including a behind-the-scenes journey of how *Goodnight Moon* came to pass. Brown was a prolific children's author at a time when the expected format of children's literature was to conform to a structured story arc with a morality message—that or a fantastical fairy tale. With *Goodnight Moon*, Brown soundly rejected this structure and adopted an altogether radical approach. She was fortunate enough to fall in with a dedicated group of avant-garde experimental writers in New York who would audition their draft stories with groups of children. Employing some unconventional brainstorming techniques, she observed that young children connected with an experience that engaged the senses and that included objects and characters they could relate to (not fantasy—this came in a later phase of childhood).

They didn't care about plot. Instead: small animals—a bunny, a mouse—and everyday objects—a comb, a brush, a lamp. These familiar objects and animals, combined with the flat, saturated, primary-hued Matisse-like illustrations of Clement Hurd and a studied focus on the sound of the rhythmic, repetitive, almost hypnotic, words, all contributed to an experience that felt just plain *good* in children's bodies. It felt comforting, safe—like a cozy blanket. And it was absolutely radical at the time—you might even say seductive.

What does this have to do with negotiation or your life? Well, it's all connected. *We* are all connected. You may be, necessarily, focused on the negotiations unfolding in your everyday life. But at the same time, throughout the centuries and continuing now, people are engaged in broader negotiations with society: challenging the status quo, asking, "Does this framework still work? Is there some other approach?" Margaret Wise Brown defied many societal rules and expectations as an individual and certainly norms in the publishing business in the 1930s through 1950s. Author of over a hundred manuscripts of children's stories, she typically worked on each for a couple of years while researching and testing language on children before she considered them complete. Ah! . . . interoception meets planning. The different schools of thought surrounding the appropriate content of children's literature remained in a standoff that lasted decades. It's hard to imagine now that we accept and cherish *Goodnight Moon*—translated into at least a dozen languages—as a mainstay of a child's bookshelf.

Sharpen your everyday negotiating superpower through planning, tuning in to your "Spidey Sense," and gazing beyond your own backyard to the larger negotiations we are witnessing right now as society evolves. It's actually terribly exciting. And if all that stimulation makes it hard to fall asleep, I can recommend a good bedtime story . . .

CHAPTER 5

TWO EARS AND ONE MOUTH: HOW TO BE THE MOST POWERFUL PERSON IN THE ROOM

When I taught the Listening module to my law students, I would ask each class for a show of hands: How many of them had been told when they were a kid that they'd make a great lawyer someday because they were a good talker or arguer? Many hands would shoot into the air. Then I'd ask how many were told they would make a great lawyer because they were a good listener. In ten years, how many hands do you think were raised in response to that prompt?

Not a single hand.

While the list of "key" negotiation skills is robust, if pressed to pick one above all others, I would single out listening—which is both terribly important and woefully underutilized. You probably talk more than you think you do. Think listening is a snooze-worthy soft skill and, besides, you're already a superstar listener? I say this with all the love and admiration in my heart for your awesomeness: Think again, Captain Fabulous. Harvard Program on Negotiation faculty member Daniel Shapiro shared in an issue of the alumni newsletter an illuminating experience from a conference call: he thought he hadn't contributed much to the conversation. But this particular conference calling service provided data on how much time each person spoke. Shapiro was surprised to discover he had actually spoken about a third more than anyone else. And that's coming from a highly trained and practiced professional (and author of *Negotiating the Nonnegotiable: How to Resolve Your Most Emotionally Charged Conflicts*).

In the early 2000s, during my initial training for the law school faculty, I learned a method for teaching listening that was developed by psychotherapist Judi MacMurray, who granted permission to share her methodology far and wide. This chapter will walk you through the heart of the materials that comprised her tutorial, supplemented by my own adaptations and experience with listening over the years. It's a painless three-step guide—not just in negotiation but in everyday conversation.

According to psychotherapists, three key traits of good listeners include being (1) nonjudgmental (see "meet them where they are," chapter 14); (2) sincere (your "insides match the outside"); and (3) empathetic (you'll notice that one repeated *ad nauseam* in these pages).

What makes listening so important?

- Listening establishes better understanding.
- Listening builds rapport, trust, and credibility.
- Listening contributes to information gathering: to negotiate a good deal, need to know what the other side wants and needs.
- Listening shows respect.

- If other side does not feel heard, they may shut down (inhibits info gathering).

- Listening buys you time and can be used as a stall tactic when you don't know what to say (think about it this way: let the burden of talking fall on them).

- Listening triggers reciprocity.

✒ Everyday Super Tip

How often do you find yourself in a conversation where the other person repeats themselves over and over like TikTok on a loop? Ever wonder why this happens? The speaker doesn't feel they've been heard. Great news! You can do something about that by practicing the technique in this chapter. Talk about a superpower—and a sanity savior!

Listening is, quite literally, the quiet superpower of everyday negotiation. Like everything else, it takes practice! Stephen Covey counseled in his book *The 7 Habits of Highly Effective People:* "Seek first to understand rather than seeking to be understood." That means prioritizing the other person's story over what you want to say. Guess what? You already know how to do this but haven't been practicing it. It's a super skill that fits the classic superhero formula— the seemingly ordinary transformed to the extraordinary. The best part is, like your trusty pocket handkerchief or most versatile lip gloss, it's a timeless, absolutely analog, and eminently portable accessory that you can deploy in everyday life at any given moment.

Step 1: Set an intention (to pay attention)
This step has two parts:

 a. *Choose to listen*—instead of fading in and out—with a purpose of understanding what the other party is saying and what makes it important to them. This means being curious. Listen for two categories: content from words and emotion—also known as the "meta" message. Choosing to listen means managing distractions.

 b. *Pay attention.* What gets in the way of this? NOISE (see Step 2)—not external, ambient noise like sirens or a barking dog but your internal noise: errands, work, a pinging phone and social media alerts, trying to remember the actor's name from that movie where they colonize Mars . . . or even just "I'm getting hungry!" Setting an intention is a *very* powerful anchor. If you don't set an intention to listen, you won't be listening effectively. You'll get bits and pieces. You might get most of what the speaker is sharing, but you won't get all of it.

Step 2: Manage your "noise" (noise = anything that distracts you)

Common Types of Noise	
Identification/ projection	"Me too."
Advice	"Been there, done that, and here's what you need to do."
The Rescuer/ co-dependency	"I'll save you!" / "I'll fix it."

Sympathy	"Oh, how terrible" (having your own feelings and wanting to express them).
Judgment	"What a stupid thing to do!" or "I can't believe she's so upset over something like this!"
Authority	"You're wrong and I know what's right" (wanting to set the speaker straight).
Interrogation	"Who did what to whom, when, and why?" (You ask questions you think are important and control the conversation.)
The Analyst	"Tell me about your childhood."
The Censor	"TMI! I don't want to hear this."
The Hummingbird	"I hope one of the kids remembered to walk the dog" (racing or spooling thoughts about other things).

S. Lucia Kanter St. Amour, *Hummingbird Noise.* Watercolor on paper.

Paying attention means (a) tracking the speaker and (b) tracking yourself. You can't eliminate your noise, but you can learn to manage it. Notice the noise and then *refocus on your intention to listen.* This is referred to as the **listening loop**. You will navigate this loop a few times while listening to someone for even just five minutes: set intention, focus, notice noise creeping in, manage noise, reset intention, etc. When you pay attention, you listen for two things: (a) words as content, and (b) feelings as content (consider feelings another category of facts). Noise pulls you away from their story and focuses on your story—e.g., thinking about what you want to say next.

> ⚡ **Everyday Super Tip**
>
> Being quiet while you wait for your turn to talk is not the same as listening.

Step 3: Reflect back

My father once told me a story about a Jesuit priest:

> *A Jesuit Provincial (a leader in the order of Jesuits) was interviewing a subordinate priest for advancement in the Order. The Provincial thoughtfully listened to the priest for about fifteen minutes as the priest summarized his loyalty to the faith, the community, and his worthiness for advancement. As he spoke, the Provincial smiled and nodded frequently. When the priest was finished speaking, the Provincial declared, "I understand. Unfortunately, the decision is not to advance you at this time." The priest was confused. "But you were smiling and nodding while I spoke." The Provincial replied, "I wanted you to feel you were being heard."*

Remaining quiet as the other person gushes, while you nod your head and then finally say, "I understand," is not really listening—at least not according to the tried-and-true protocol I'm teaching here. How do you know you understand? How do *they* know you understand? Maybe you misunderstood something. Maybe their thoughts aren't organized and they haven't expressed themselves accurately. You could each, literally or figuratively, be perceiving the situation in different languages (but similar enough to go undetected). An experienced Danish attorney and negotiator shared with me how similar—but different in many important ways—the Danish and Swedish languages are. He had been party to a few situations where each side to the negotiation thought they understood one another and had closed a deal, only to later realize they had divergent understandings of the deal.

The job of a skilled listener could be described as helping the talker talk. By reflecting back (that is, summarizing the essence of both words and emotions - *why* the speaker cares), you accomplish a few things:

- **Empathy** (the ability to understand and share the feelings of another)
- **Clarification** ("No, that's not what I meant. I meant . . . ")
- **Verification** ("Yes, that's right! You got it.")
- **Encouragement** (which gets you even more information)
- **De-escalation** (and slowing down the excretion of cortisol in the speaker's brain. Cortisol is a stress hormone that the brain cranks out and can really derail things. More on this in chapter 11.)

IT'S OK IF YOU REFLECT BACK AND YOU GET IT WRONG. For one thing, you're already showing the speaker that you are listening. Also, reflecting helps *them* be more clear in communicating, and it's an opportunity for them to clarify.

"What if I can't keep track of it all or I don't know what to say to reflect back?"

Don't panic. You almost CAN'T do this wrong. If faced with the full tilt speaker who doesn't allow for pauses and natural reflection points, let that little steel ball dart around the pinball machine. It won't persist indefinitely, and that's what they need to do. Don't worry about remembering it all. When they do surface from their heightened state (and they will), reflect back the *essence* of what you heard—especially points and words that were repeated. Their "gush" will gradually ebb after each round of reflecting back and their verification or clarification (and additional speaking). I recall a carpool commute to a conference with a work colleague with whom I was friendly but not especially close. He was navigating a heart-wrenching personal ordeal and decided that my captive audience in a car was the perfect opportunity to unburden himself. He spilled out his troubles to a degree that wasn't exactly proportionate to the scope of our relationship, but there we were huddled together in a Fiat 500 and tethered to traffic. I didn't know what to say, so I didn't say much of anything at all (this differs from waiting quietly for my turn to talk. See "stall tactic" above. Other than managing my "censor" noise, it's an apt example of letting the burden of talking fall on the speaker). Once he finished his gush, he fell quiet for about twenty seconds, a silence I did not fill (see chapter 3). Finally, he exhaled and announced, "Wow. You're a great listener. Thanks. It means a lot to me!" Then we listened to music for the remainder of the trip.

While my carpool example doesn't conform with this listening protocol, it does demonstrate the power of silence and giving another person the space to freely express themselves, which can have a meaningful impact in everyday negotiation. If reflecting back is challenging for you and all you can do for starters is just repeat back the last one to three words the speaker said, you'd be amazed at just how effective an everyday hack that can be. It works something like this:

SPEAKER: "I'm so frustrated I can't get my toddler to eat her peas!"

YOU: "Eat her peas . . ."

SPEAKER: "Yes! She only eats white foods—vanilla yogurt, string cheese, bananas. She needs vegetables!"

YOU: "Vegetables . . ."

SPEAKER: "Exactly! I'm such a health and fitness fanatic and I have a child whose diet isn't nutritious . . ."

(Now we're getting somewhere)

Notice what is *not* included in our adroit three-step listening algorithm, with one exception that I'm about to share:

Asking questions!

Wanting to ask questions actually qualifies as a type of noise that distracts you from the speaker and requires you to reset your initial intention. But when it seems like the speaker is "done," and after you have gone through a few cycles of reflecting back and getting clarification or verification—nope, it's still not your turn—you then ask what I call a *Super Stealth Question*:

✓ Super Stealth Question #1

"Is there anything else?"

So often this simple little question—strategically posed at what *appears to be* the end of the listening and speaking cycle—exposes some rich little nugget that may have otherwise remained incognito. There's another "super stealth question" when it comes to negotiating in general, but I'm saving it for later.

Think of your goal like this: to listen to that other person like they have never been listened to before. You concede nothing by doing this; understanding somebody does not mean you agree with them. For a demonstration of this listening model in action, check out episode 8 of my podcast *Forces of Good: The Superpower of Everyday Negotiation* (available on Substack and Apple Podcasts).

Like other negotiation skills, listening isn't a superpower unless you practice and develop it. The three-step technique might feel uncomfortable and come across awkwardly at first. One does not perform *The Marriage of Figaro* without having mastered *Twinkle Twinkle Little Star.* So you might start off using this model with close friends and family. You can be transparent: "Hey, I read this totally spellbinding best-selling book on negotiation, and the author teaches this method of listening, and I'm trying it out." If you keep it up, you'll become so seamless people won't notice that you are employing a "technique." You might become such a natural that even you forget you're following steps.

I have actually been in several negotiations in my legal career where I have demonstrated listening to the party on the other side of the bargaining table better than their own attorney has. And guess what that made me?

The most powerful person in the room.

Finally, I'm reminded of the wise old proverb that points out we have two ears and one mouth and we should use them in that proportion. Easier said than done, but it's doable—and immensely potent. It all starts with setting the intention . . .

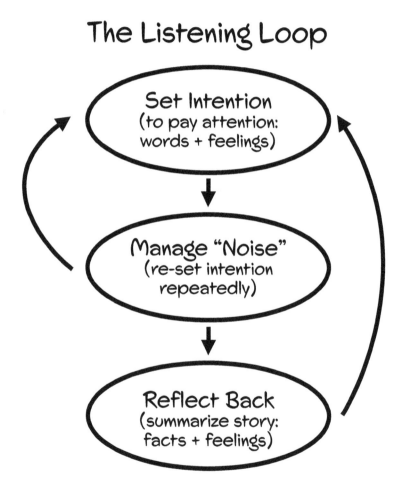

The Listening Loop

Set Intention
(to pay attention:
words + feelings)

Manage "Noise"
(re-set intention
repeatedly)

Reflect Back
(summarize story:
facts + feelings)

CHAPTER 6

THE CAT RIDDLE: PERSPECTIVE-SHIFTING AND IMAGINATION IN NEGOTIATION

During the 2020 COVID shelter-in-place orders, when people were glued to social media for tips on sourdough starters and DIY haircuts, a short riddle circulated that exemplifies what I would call another "secret in plain sight" for more sophisticated negotiating (in addition to agility, mentioned previously).

First, the riddle: In a square room there is a cat in every corner. In front of every cat there are three cats. How many cats are there in all?

Hint: It is not a math problem.

The key to solving the riddle is in *perspective-shifting*. Experienced mediators are able to solve this riddle in fairly short order because we are trained in perspective-shifting (more on mediators and mediation in later chapters). What does that mean? The concept is simple though, like everything else, requires practice to be effective: When working through a problem, examine it—and possible solutions—from various angles. Ask not only "How might a judge view the situation?" but "How could an engineer view it?" An accountant? A grade school teacher? A nurse? A real estate broker? A hotel manager? Note: this is different from imagining *yourself* in another person's shoes, which is not true perspective shifting. In this way, according to David Rock, co-founder and executive director of the Neuroleadership Institute, empathy is incorrectly taught.

Imagining the question or problem from that of an objective third party *in a particular position* may prove easier than conjuring the perspective of the other specific players in the negotiation, depending upon the degree of emotions and biases in play. Perspective-shifting is a technique that can break through impasses, dodge personal biases, help save face, and inspire proposals for durable and pragmatic solutions. And the best part is that one doesn't need a credential in engineering, accounting, teaching, nursing, investment brokerage, or even being a cat to employ the technique.

An old joke (possibly dating to the 1920s, though its origin is in dispute) illustrates how parties can often feel and behave when stuck on their own narrative—their own perspective. It tells of a police officer who comes across a drunken man intently searching the ground near a lamppost. The officer asks him the goal of his quest. The inebriate replies that he is looking for his car keys, and the officer helps for a few minutes without success, then asks whether the man is certain that he dropped the keys near the lamppost. "No," is the reply, "I lost the keys somewhere across the street." "Then why are looking over here?" asks the perplexed officer. "The light is much better here," the intoxicated man responds.

⚡ Everyday Super Tip

Look around, up, down, diagonally—get a step stool and a plumber's snake if needed. Failure to explore places other than where you find it convenient and comfortable to see the world will often leave you stuck in the same place.

On that note, consider the cat riddle from the perspective of the cat: If a cat occupies one of the corners facing into the square room, what does it see? From that vantage point, it sees the three other cats "in front of" it. Thus, assuming the law of gravity applies, and that no cats occupy the four corners of the ceiling, the answer is . . .

(*Do not read past this sentence if you are still trying to work it out on your own.*)

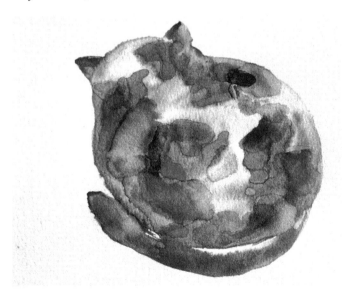

S. Lucia Kanter St. Amour, *Cat Perspective.*
Watercolor and distressed ink on paper.

Four.

Solving the cat riddle, like examining any problem from a different perspective, requires *imagination*.

In his book *Sapiens: A Brief History of Humankind*, Yuval Noah Harari affirms that the greatest advantage held by Homo sapiens in the evolutionary process is our imagination capacity: the ability to create fiction and believe in common myths. Harari points out that a large number of strangers may efficiently cooperate among themselves when they believe in the same myths. He suggests that this assumption applies to both the modern state and to ancient tribes; in both cases, the shared myths exist only in the collective imagination.

Anthropologists think that for about 190,000 of our first years as Homo sapiens, we mostly used imagination to resolve disputes and solve problems. On the southeastern African savannas, small migrating bands of hunter-gatherers sat around campfires and combined their imaginations to invent the best ways to survive. While they did not invent the fire that warmed them, cooked their food, and protected them, they did invent an impressive list of ways to use it. Around those campfires humans used their collective imaginations and their long-term relationships to survive and develop even better ways to live.

Yet somehow modern adult humans have stifled these interactive skills that promoted our success as a species, not in small part due to three distinct industrial revolutions throughout the centuries and the technology explosion, which automates process and decision-making, purportedly making everything "easier." But this artificial intelligence and other digital modalities designed to "simplify" things may come at the cost of eroding the human cognitive process of imagination. After all, if a packaged solution is built into an app, why continue thinking through alternatives?

It's different in children, who frequently engage in pretend play with one another. Pretend play activities help children to adopt the role of somebody or something else. This modality is essential not only because it fires up their creativity and imagination, but also because it helps to develop critical skills such as communication, empathy, and socialization. Through this type of play activity, kids can learn different talents and attitudes. They will also become adept at expressing their feelings and building language and motion skills.

Clearly, the capacity for imagination was decisive in the formation and organization of human society for both bonding and its opposite—divisiveness. In contemporary history, trust is placed on fictional constructs, such as market, economy, currency, institutional prestige, and corporations, among others. They owe their validity, efficiency, and legal personality to a social consensus based on fiction. Commerce, empires, and universal religion are fictions that led us to today's globalized world—and are responsible for many wars. Individuals and groups who share a mythology or belief system become an in-group that perceives shared values and goals. They trust each other, which is crucial to work collaboratively to achieve shared goals and solve problems.

But too much conformity—and association with only like-minded people—without continuing to feed the imagination—can keep us from making progress. The most successful among us, throughout history, have been a little rebellious. They break conventions. Rather than wrapping themselves in the security blanket of the status quo, they change the world with unconventional thinking (consider Margaret Wise Brown from chapter 4, Steve Jobs, Harriet Tubman,

Jane Goodall, Julia Child, Malala Yousafzai, and Che Guevara). As Francesca Gino argues in her captivating leadership book *Rebel Talent*, the future belongs to the rebel—and there's a rebel in each of us.

⚡ Everyday Super Tip

Remember the giant paper clip from chapter 3? In your preparation stage, get creative without censoring yourself. Think not just "outside the box." Think, "What box?" Later, as you continue the negotiation process, you will cull the creative ideas and match them with needs, interests, and practical considerations and test them for durability. You never know when a seemingly zany idea could lead to an implementable breakthrough.

Imagination, or inventing a fiction, also serves as an important tool to boost one's confidence, aspirations, and willingness to even enter into a negotiation at all. Plenty of research has shown that negotiators with strong alternatives are able to secure a more satisfying agreement. But lesser-known and lesser-discussed research suggests that you don't necessarily need to have an attractive alternative; *you just need to think that you do*.

Mentally simulating an attractive alternative can make you a better negotiator. From the neuroscience angle, imagining a workable alternative will slow the cerebral cortisol-spiking associated with feelings of helplessness in the planning stages and the negotiation itself, thus diminishing the prospect that the brain's executive functioning will shut down (more on this in chapter 11). Athletes have engaged the imagination for years as part of training and competition: using visualization techniques, they imagine in their mind's eye the perfect trajectory (of a free throw, an approach shot with a 9 iron to the green, a tennis serve) before performing the real thing.

✎ Everyday Super Tip

Use your mind's eye as a metaverse portal: vividly and specifically imagining and believing an outcome can increase your chances of realizing it—or an approximation of it.

How is this useful in negotiating? In short, imagination is an incredibly powerful evolutionary process for invention, social bonding, and problem solving. Understanding the anthropological, behavioral economic, and neuro-scientific importance of imagination; making an effort to discover other people's beliefs and fictions with genuine curiosity (you don't have to agree with them); and relating those beliefs to the way people make decisions can be an incredibly effective tool in negotiation.

As a mediator, at some point in any given mediation, I am known to pose a question to the parties that begins with *Imagine if* . . . and it is remarkable how this simple framework can free the mind and emotions from staying stuck in their own narrative and can break through a perceived impasse to hatch and explore untapped possibilities.

As David Pogue of *The New York Times* shared, "You've never seen a cat skeleton in a tree, have you?" He was referring to when a reader's cat couldn't get down from a tree, and her grandmother reassured her with those words, predicting—correctly—that the cat would not indefinitely remain stuck in the tree. "This advice made me realize that, sometimes, you need to shift your perception of a problem to see a solution," the reader noted.

S. Lucia Kanter St. Amour, *Rebel Thought Garden.* Watercolor on paper.

CHAPTER 7

THE 1998 HOSTAGE CRISIS: NEGOTIATING WHEN THERE'S NO PLAN

Now I take you back in time to August of 1998. I traveled in Russia, via London, with my parents after just taking the grueling three-day California Bar Exam. I had spent the final semester of law school learning Russian because I have a policy of trying to learn the language of the country I'm visiting; it seems like a basic courtesy, and I have no qualms about performing an activity badly in front of other people. That's how you build skills—by doing them awkwardly to start.

In London on my way to St. Petersburg, I met up with a law school buddy. We had tea at Fortnum & Mason, shopped antiques at Portobello Road, and visited the Tower of London. We did the law geek tour and visited the Old Bailey, the civil court, and the House of Commons, and took a day trip out to Hampton Court—where we got lost in the famous hedge maze but then cleverly figured out the "secret" to the maze and found our way back to civilization.

When I finally arrived in St. Petersburg, I was delighted to find that the fax (yes . . . a facsimile) I had sent from a travel agency in

London in an attempt to prearrange an airport taxi had actually worked: A man dutifully stood bearing a sign with my name, just like you see in the movies—well, and in real life at the airport . . . and I was reunited with my parents, who had arrived the previous day.

We weren't traveling with any group tour. We were on our own, as all three of us had extensive international travel experience. That turned out to be a mistake. Russia in 1998 was maybe 10 percent "open" to tourism, with incongruent information making it tough to tour independently. Getting around was difficult, communication was difficult (my Russian language lessons saved us!), and even securing food was difficult. Prices were high, comforts were minimal, freedom of movement was not encouraged, and the economy was clearly troubled. With the exceptions of the area surrounding the Hermitage Museum, it was a place mired in poverty and disrepair. And the Russian people seemed downtrodden. With each passing day, we became so fatigued and discouraged that we finally marched into a travel agency to find out about any group tours we could join.

As it turned out, one of the Volga River cruise ships to Moscow had one cabin available. The catch was that there wasn't a single English speaker on the ship; it was a cruise full of tourists from Barcelona, so the only languages spoken by passengers and interpreters were Russian and Spanish. "No problem," I assured my parents—I spoke both those languages.

That was when our real adventure began.

So, off we went to the Metro to eventually arrive at the port where we would embark.

A REMINISCENCE OF THE ST. PETERSBURG METRO
Mayakovskaya station, taken directly from my 1998 travel journal:

*It was like something out of that movie, Blade Runner—
downright Orwellian. It is grim inside and very very
crowded. You buy a token and then drop the token into
a turnstile, which places you at the top of a long escalator. We got on the escalator and rode, I am <u>not kidding</u>,
for about a quarter of a mile (!!) underground. These
crazy dim cone-shaped lights hover above you. No one is
talking and there is somehow a menacing ambiance. I
felt a little nervous, but was glad we were with the travel
agent, Tanya. I asked Tanya if the Metro was dangerous
at night; she looked me in the eyes and responded with
one word, "Da!" [that's a YES]. Once we reached the bottom, it was like we had descended into the underworld.
Dark and silent and cold. There were no visible tracks—
only a series of elevator-type doors with clumps of people
waiting in front of each set of doors. No one spoke. It was
eerily devoid of chatter or human interaction. Without
Tanya I would have not had any idea what to do. But, we
stood and waited with a particular clump. Suddenly, the
doors in front of us opened revealing a stopped train car.
We were shoved inside by the throng of people around us,
and the doors slammed shut. Thus, we were inside a concrete tube. This was around the time when I just wanted
to get the hell out of there. I felt trapped. Eventually, we
alighted at the river harbor Okukhovo stop and ascended
the long long escalator for our ¼ mile ride to the top.*

We then walked a couple of blocks to the seaport, where all the cruise ships were lined up. The long and short of it is that I spent the next nine days interpreting between Spanish, Russian, and English for my parents. It was cold. It rained practically every day. I became exhausted. As our cruise down the Volga to Moscow drew to a close, my parents were interested in exiting Russia via train, which would take us through Ukraine, and we thought we would need to apply for special visas, according to something my mom had read in a travel book. Bear in mind our entire original travel itinerary had been turned upside down, so we were winging it at this point.

That was when my mom took it upon herself to negotiate with the cruise director, Ludmila, who, again, spoke not a word of English—about looking into tickets to commute us through Ukraine and onward somewhere else. Recall chapter 3 where I caution about bringing the right people to the negotiation . . .

I'm not sure what transpired, as my dad and I had scurried off on our own excursion. But when we returned, I immediately detected from my mother's countenance that something had gone awry in our absence. Ludmila, most likely planning to inflate any quote she procured so that she could pocket a little fee for her efforts, offered to inquire into the train tickets and visa on our behalf. My mom insists she made it clear to Ludmila that she did not want her to purchase any tickets; she only asked for information. I'm guessing this last crucial point was lost in translation, because Ludmila had purchased train tickets for us through Ukraine and was demanding that we pay her a sum representing the cost of the tickets plus a 50 percent markup as a "service fee" for her efforts.

My mom had awaited my return to leverage my interpreting services and to help Ludmila understand her mistake purchasing tickets, the unsupportable metric for her service fee—even if we could use the tickets—and the futility of the train tickets due to the visa required to pass through Ukraine. I spent the next hour or so trying to reason with Ludmila, with the help of one of the Russian–Spanish interpreters on the ship. The ensuing theater included actual fist-shaking, foot-stomping, and paper-throwing on the part of Ludmila, accompanied by her refusal to acknowledge any misunderstanding or error. We steadfastly refused to yield and to pay. From our perspective, it was a shakedown.

The next morning, all of the Barcelona passengers had disembarked the vessel (for good) around 5:00 a.m.—as did all of the interpreters. The only remaining passengers were my parents and me. We woke up a bit later and packed our bags to also leave the ship for our next destination (not yet known). But when we attempted to leave, Ludmila appeared, began shouting at us, and summoned three uniformed men with rifles to block our path. She disembarked from the ship and returned with the captain of the neighboring ship and three more men. They closed off the exits and locked us inside with them. Ludmila and the captain disembarked.

And there we were: held hostage at gunpoint. And by whom? Port authority? We didn't know the significance of the uniforms. But we understood the rifles.

At this point you might be thinking, "Why are you telling this story? This is supposed to be a book about the superpower of *everyday* negotiation. This is an extraordinary event that hardly happens every day to the common person. But wait . . .

While this is, admittedly, a vivid and extreme example, it's something that happens in everyday life all the time: feeling you've been backed into a corner—physically or figuratively—unprepared, with no plan, and needing to think and act quickly to negotiate your way through the situation.

Now I'll let you in on another bonus of preparing a planning memo as a habit before any negotiation: It actually trains your mind and skills to be a more spontaneous actor and think quickly on your feet in situations where you haven't had the benefit of planning. At the time of this incident in 1998, I didn't yet have all the years of practicing law, teaching, and international lecturing experience as a subject matter expert in negotiation that I have now. All I had at my disposal were those same lemonade-stand instincts from the 1981 garage sale (well, that and a few more years of life experience and a law degree).

So, what would you have done next in this situation? What was our next play? Locked in, isolated on a ship, rifles trained on us . . .

My 1998 Matryoshka (Russian Nesting Dolls)

CHAPTER 8

RUNNING FROM RUSSIA: STORYTELLING IN NEGOTIATION

When I aired the Russia hostage episodes of my podcast, I split it into two episodes, the first episode ending with that "cliffhanger" and inviting listeners to write in with their suggestions for how they would have handled it. Some of the advice I received included:

> *Rush at the guards all at once to catch them off guard, overtake and disarm them.*
>
> *Run in three different directions on the ship.*
>
> *Pretend to have a seizure of some medical emergency to get them to open the doors.*
>
> *Bribe them.*

Well, this is what we did:

Nothing.

We ignored them . . . and waited them out.

> ### ⚡ Everyday Super Tip
>
> Doing nothing might be your next move in a negotiation as well. Inaction can be a form of action. We'll explore this more in chapter 12.

Oddly, I didn't feel afraid. Perhaps it was just a defense mechanism or the naïveté of youth. But it helped me keep my wits about me. As well traveled as I was at age twenty-seven, my father was much more so and was not feeling the same equanimity; plus, he had a bad cold and needed to lie down. I got the feeling our captors didn't exactly answer to Ludmila and were just as surprised as we were to be co-opted and put on the spot. I also wondered whether their shift would end and they'd have other places to be—or at least not want to stick around not getting paid. Ludmila, for her part, had bailed.

I proffered to my parents in a calm, low voice, "Look. These guys probably have to report somewhere at some point. They can't just hang out here indefinitely. We can. We have no place we need to be. So, let's just sit tight and be the happy, friendly, nonthreatening American family." Although I was not at that point trained in negotiation analysis as I am today, I now recognize that, while the asymmetry in power favored them, the asymmetry of time favored us (see chapter 1 and the third round of chocolate negotiations). My mom seconded that strategy and also agreed to say the words "American Embassy" every few sentences.

So, that's what we did. We sat down on the floor, chatted among ourselves (I think my dad actually stretched out and closed his eyes), and shrugged our shoulders a lot as if to signal, "No idea what's going on. Some sort of misunderstanding." After a couple of hours, the men with the rifles became restless and annoyed. They started whispering among themselves and then finally—abruptly—unlocked the door and motioned for us—with their rifles, mind you—to exit. We rose and disembarked.

Once we reached the concrete concourse, that's when I got scared. Wide-open space surrounded us as we retreated, and I feared we might be shot in the back. We scampered toward the freeway and hailed a cab. We poured ourselves into the taxi and asked the driver to ferry us to freedom (or at least to the American Express office). Along the way, we observed locals making runs on the banks with armed police presence, though we didn't make sense of that until the next day when we came across an English newspaper. When we arrived at American Express, we requested passage out of the country ASAP, our depleted sense of safety and security precariously perched on the Formica counter that separated us from the impassive agent. She found a flight departing for Budapest in three hours. Sold.

The following day in Budapest we learned that the ruble had crashed, and President Boris Yeltsin had sacked his government the day before our departure—the very day we were at the Kremlin ourselves.

And now for the punch line. It was 2018 when I came across my Russia travel journal. My younger son was thirteen. My father was visiting for Christmas, and, together, we told him this story for the first time. My father's and my accounts of the events, after twenty years, were remarkably similar—practically identical. My son listened in silence to the whole story and then asked one simple question. It was a question that had not occurred to me in 1998, nor since. His question was:

"How much money were they asking for?"

I didn't know! I turned to my dad: "Dad? How much was it?"

My father's response: "Oh. About five hundred dollars."

Me: "Wait . . . What? Five . . ."

Dad: "I don't negotiate with terrorists!"

OK, Dad. Noted. Good to know . . .

> ## 〽 Everyday Super Tip
>
> If you take away nothing else from this book, this is the one nugget I hope you remember. If your family is taken hostage and $500 cash (adjusting for inflation, let's say about $850) will resolve that situation . . . *pay the money and get out of there.*

Was it a shakedown? Sure it was! But there are times when standing on principle is not the play. Remember the chocolate negotiations from chapter 1? Remember the students who rejected the unfair offer of just one out of the ten chocolates as insulting, even though their sole job was to get chocolate? One chocolate is better than no chocolates. Five hundred dollars for your family's safety and security? Sounds like a bargain!

Now, what was the point of all that? What have I been doing throughout this chapter and, indeed, starting with the very preface of this book?

I told you a story.

I talked a little bit about the magic of storytelling in chapter 4 and how pioneering *Goodnight Moon* author Margaret Wise Brown was in the 1940s with the sensory-focused language she introduced to children's literature. She tapped into something in young children . . . something visceral that got under their skin and captivated them. Turns out, storytelling can play a role in everyday negotiation—and we all have stories to share!

Early in my legal career, I found myself in a typical settlement negotiation with opposing counsel in a case involving an employee suing for wrongful termination. We had been at the table for a couple of hours cautiously trading information, each attempting to persuade the other to see how the law, or a jury, would favor our respective clients and why our negotiation demand was reasonable and meritorious. At one point, we seemed stuck, and, at least in my mind, it appeared as though we would leave the table that day without a deal. The other attorney, who had quite a bit more experience than I did, suddenly announced, "Let me tell you a story." Without waiting for permission, he launched into a narrative about negotiating for a rug while on a trip visiting Istanbul. I set my pen down and settled in to hear him out. Where was he going with this? And how would the story end? He had my attention, and I always love a good story.

He unspooled his tale about how the rug merchant had served him tea, and they sat and talked about their families, and how he thoughtfully looked through the inventory, pausing to ask about various rugs, with the merchant proudly explaining in detail the craftsmanship of each of them, before narrowing in on one of them, and then more tea was poured, and the merchant even threw tea on the rug to show that the dyes were good quality and would not bleed. The haggling over price eventually developed. He recounted how he and the rug merchant went back and forth on price for a while, until they finally reached a number that they could both agree upon.

At that point, he told the merchant (about an hour into their repartee), "Yes. That is a good price. That would, indeed, be a good price for me. But you see, this rug is actually for my son. My son is just starting out in his career and asked me to select a rug for his new home with his new bride, and he is on a less forgiving budget than I am. So, we need to reach a price that is good for my son," and the negotiation continued "on behalf of his son." It was actually a charming little story, and we were both smiling as it drew to a close. We picked up where we had left off with our own negotiation and were able to each find more wiggle room for a deal.

What I did not understand at the time was that my more seasoned counterpart knew how to cast a storytelling "spell" to lubricate the gears of dealmaking. In 2021, Joshua Weiss, cofounder of the Global Negotiation Initiative, spoke on a Harvard Law School Program On Negotiation webinar about the power of story in negotiation, which is often more about creativity than it is about compromise. Stories are a way of assimilating creativity into a negotiation and can be pivotal for a variety of reasons:

- Good stories create a sense of connection. When someone says, "I have a story to tell you," people are intrigued and **more open to listening**. They invite the listener into the story, making them more curious and open to learning— "What else might be going on here that I didn't think about when preparing?" They can also convey complex ideas in ways that are easy to grasp.

- People are **less likely to interrupt** a story than they are when you list all the reasons for your demands. It also makes them wonder, "What will happen next?"

- Stories are **extremely effective at building rapport** and tend to reveal commonalities, which makes it much easier to transcend positions and discover underlying interests. They can also help save face when a party to the negotiation has gotten themselves in a trap with their own behavior, and can break an impasse.

- Stories transcend different learning styles, convey lessons, and provide **relatable examples**.

- Stories are disarming and **nurturing**—reminiscent of a parent reading a bedtime story. Importantly, they often come from an outside perspective, which can help foster trust. That is, you aren't making it about you. Oddly, even when you are telling a story about yourself, it seems to come from someplace else.

- Stories are excellent **memory aids** and easier to recall in tense moments than data. The story about haggling for the rug in Istanbul? That was told to me in the year 2000 and I never wrote it down (until now, in 2022), but I remembered it after all this time.

- Stories are **normative**. They comfort people by reminding them that this isn't the only time someone has dealt with this kind of a challenge. Others have figured it out, and so can we.

- Stories are **hard to argue with**—they can't be debated or discredited by the other side. This is important because, although *you can't change people's minds* in a situation where the parties hold two opposing ideologies, *telling a story might cause them to change their own mind.*

Finally, it's worth mentioning the internal negotiation: What story are you telling yourself about the negotiation, and how might that be holding you back? Can you change your story? For example, are you telling yourself, "I have no power here" (see final chapter)? Examining your own story can help level a power imbalance. Consider the example of a single company that has the very specialized equipment you need. Can you improve your alternatives in some way you have not considered and that the other party, who thinks they have a hold over you, also hasn't considered (see chapter 6—using imagination)? Can you build your own mousetrap? Can you rent it, recycle it, reverse-engineer it? You might consult an outside third party for a perspective—or even just watch a true-life-inspired underdog sports movie (*ahem,* stories!)—for some inspiration (*Miracle, Moneyball, Secretariat,* and *A League of Their Own* are a few of my favorites).

The bottom line is that stories are universal. Every culture on the planet has a history of stories. Storytelling is ancient; there is no stronger connection between people. Stories create bonds between people, emphasize shared values and goals, and bridge differences. This is how deals are sealed and conflicts are healed.

✐ Everyday Super Tip

Remember story time at the public library? Next time you are preparing for a negotiation (or even a difficult conversation with somebody), have a story or two in your quiver that you can share at the right moment to build rapport, ease a tense moment, break through an impasse, or spur the other side's sense of curiosity so that you are both more open to listening and learning from each other.

CHAPTER 9

RAGING BULL vs. ATTICUS FINCH: THE LANGUAGE WE USE IN NEGOTIATION

S. Lucia Kanter St. Amour, *Eavesdropping.*
Watercolor and colored pencil on paper.

When I received a monthly invoice for my brick-and-mortar office share with an increase that I had not agreed to, that nobody had even talked to me about, I was confused. In fact, due to the repeated mishandling of my mail a few years earlier, which resulted in donation checks for my nonprofit organization and court notices being returned to the sender, I had reached a settlement with the management company for a discounted rate going forward, which was to be indefinite. I sent the office manager an email asking for clarification on this new bill and whether it was, perhaps, just a mistake. An email rally ensued. On the one hand, she denied any knowledge of my settlement, and on the other hand, she claimed to have been the owner of the business for the past ten years, meaning she would have approved any such agreement. I noticed she wouldn't simply answer my question. I proposed a phone conversation and asked her to please review the past records surrounding the settlement, which I forwarded to her for her convenience.

When we finally connected on the phone in synchronous time, she immediately hijacked the discourse with a monologue about how she had told her family at the dinner table that she had gone "head to head" with a "high-powered" attorney who went to "Stanford" and who was a negotiation expert . . . she went on to say that I had gotten my "pound of flesh" from them these past five years with a "cheap" rate I'd "beaten" out of them for the "alleged" mishandling of mail—and she was quick to insist that, in her experience, complaints about mishandling of mail were almost never their fault—and that it was time for me to pay my "fair share."

My interoception (see chapter 4) informed me I was under attack.

Remember Axelrod's lessons from chapter 2? He admonished starting off by being cooperative. She was not. She had decided ahead of time that she was going to take charge of this discussion and put me in my place. So I made a quick calculation to match her strategy, according to Axelrod's "tit-for-tat" protocol. I used an intentionally quiet tone to contrast with her bombastic one and called her out:

"Wow. I don't know quite what to do with that. First of all, I didn't go to Stanford. I'm not sure where you're getting your information."

(Side note: I attended UC Berkeley, aka "Cal," for my undergraduate degree. GO BEARS!)

"Second, I have no idea what you mean by 'high-powered attorney.' What *do* you mean?"

Pause. No response. I let the silence sit for a few seconds to make her squirm because I doubted she had even thought about it at all. I continued:

"I'm a mediator, a peace-builder—and when I do represent a client, it usually means someone homeless who lost their apartment after not making the rent due to a job injury because the employer refused to report it to the workers comp carrier and told them too bad because they are an undocumented worker, and they had to give up their kids to foster care. Those are my clients.

"Third, the way you're speaking to me to start off this conversation is so full of aggressive and negating—and frankly just reductive and offensive language—it makes me wonder if you googled 'How to talk to a high-powered attorney.' And finally, I certainly should not be important enough to feature as the topic of dinner conversation with your family. I think this has really gotten off on the wrong footing. Let's try again."

And then I asked her if she'd had a chance to review the records I'd sent her before the call. She had not. Ah! So, she hadn't even bothered to prepare. She was ready for a fight—to battle and beat the "high-powered attorney" so she could report that back at the dinner table. This was so dehumanizing. I wasn't going to fight.

By the way, the bottom line is that, by the end of that fifteen-minute call, I did agree to a rate increase.

Of five dollars a month.

The office manager's diatribe was so marked by disrespectful, careless, combative language; assumptions; and lack of preparation, curiosity, rapport-building; information-gathering, empathy . . . need I go on? Her approach was the very antithesis of everything I'm trying to impart in this book.

It made me think about the language we use: with each other in everyday life, about one another with other people, and of course in negotiation.

Let's start with the word *fight*. I hear that all the time in contexts where I think what people really mean is *advocate*. "Fighting" for a cause, "fighting" for a result, "fighting" for progress, even "fighting" for peace. *Fight* is everywhere. It's sloppy. It's thoughtless. It sets a combative tone. We hear versions of it in so many contexts: the battle of the sexes, the war on drugs, sparring for a job promotion, clawing for resources, "armed" for a family gathering . . .

I will confess something so as to be clear about who I am: I'm Atticus Finch, not Jake LaMotta. I'm not really a fighter. I'm an advocate. I started off my career in litigation—the legal term for fighting—and it devoured me. I was dreadfully unhappy. I suffered stomachaches, headaches, insomnia. Although I'm grateful for the "boot camp" and the skills it taught me, it was also the place my soul went to die. I left litigation after four years.

As in the conversation with the office manager, I still find myself vexed at the casually provocative and even hurtful language that people bandy about within communities and workplaces. I served in a board of directors position in 2021 in a very white, male, conservative environment—really, I can explain (see chapter 15)—where I was also the only attorney on the board. I scrutinized the organization's bylaws, policies, and protocols, and acted on specific and reasonable diversity, equity, and inclusion steps to nudge them forward from the early twentieth century. To say my agenda was met with resistance is a polite understatement and—here's the kicker—the other directors kept using the word *fight* to describe my efforts. I kept correcting them: "I'm not fighting. I'm advocating. There's a big difference." But they weren't hearing it. Oh, and here's a little negotiation insight: if you find yourself needing to explain, you've probably already lost your cause.

Here are some other words and phrases (many in writing) that were used to describe me in my 2021 diversity, equity, and inclusion (DE&I) effort and for other disconcerting conduct on my part—such as regularly showing up for committee meetings and insisting that meeting minutes be prepared and posted:

- Controlling
- Pushy
- Omnipresent
- Like Mom is in the room making sure everyone plays nice
- Manipulative

- Power hungry
- Complicated (see chapter 11)
- Feisty
- There seems to be a lot of drama
- Intense

That list is illustrative, rated for a general audience, and not exhaustive. I had enough evidence and examples of written and spoken language to and about me to confirm the messaging along the lines of: "Lucia, why are you stirring up all this trouble? You were chosen for this position to be just enough out of your depth to smile, to nod in agreement, and to look pretty in your Italian heels. You're not playing along." Sure, I can rock a pointy-toe slingback with the best of them, but I can do so much more! At one point in a meeting as I held fast on a particular initiative that represented equity and inclusion for women in the organization and how it mattered for progress, retention, and attracting future customers, one of the other directors growled, "You're being such an attorney!" Again, I was reduced to a trope and chided for overstepping. It happens all the time. I believe it is an effort to simplify a situation or person that confuses or upsets them. It especially happens when the status quo of their environment is challenged.

In chapter 11 we'll learn what experts say about human behavior when someone invades their tribe with ideas that are perceived as "complicated." Plato warned us about this dynamic as early as 380 BCE with his *Allegory of the Cave*. The allegory, narrated by Socrates, is a dialogue ruminating on belief versus knowledge. A group of people have lived chained to the wall of a cave all their lives, facing a blank wall. The people can see shadows projected on the wall from objects passing in front of a fire behind them and assign names to these shadows. The shadows are their reality. They don't understand them as mere fragments of reality and not accurate representations of the real world. One of the cave prisoners manages to free himself and escapes the cave to understand and perceive the higher levels of reality. The emancipated prisoner thinks the world outside the cave is fuller and superior to the world he knew in the cave and attempts to share this with the cave community, inviting them onto the journey. But the eyes of the returning prisoner, now accustomed to the sunlight, were blinded upon reentering the cave, just as they were when first exposed to the sun. The cave dwellers, inferring from their compadre's blindness that the journey out of the cave had caused harm and perceiving the returning prisoner as dangerous with his ideas, decide no one should undertake a similar journey. They try to kill him and resolve to attempt to kill anyone else who tries to leave the cave.

As a podcast host and writer, I understand the importance of vivid language that engages the audience, that helps them conjure an image in their minds. But in social interactions, in work relationships, in negotiation, think about how you might be more thoughtful with language—not just to others but with yourself. There are times in life when it is necessary and right to fight. That's litigation. This is a book on the superpower of everyday *negotiation*, and choosing your words carefully is part of honing that particular power.

Contrasting the action-packed "fight" vocabulary, now let's look at a mundane and innocuous-looking little word: *but*.

"But" tends to negate whatever came before it. Let's drop it into an example of reflecting what you hear someone say during a negotiation (chapter 5) to see how this operates:

"It sounds like you've given considerable thought to a creative proposal, **but** it could use some additional elaboration."

The word *but* almost screams, "Nice try, but not good enough," and hinders the process from moving forward. Now substitute the word *and* for *but*. Notice how it transforms the reflection into something encouraging, and frames it as a joint effort for both parties to work on together.

"It sounds like you've given considerable thought to a creative proposal, **and** it could use some additional elaboration."

Much like the "Why" questions—see chapter 10—I make an effort to avoid the conjunction *but* and replace it with *and* in mediations and negotiations—unless I really mean it—that is, I intend to negate the preceding clause. As cautioned by the Benjen Stark character in *Game of Thrones*, episode 3 season 1, "Anything you say before the word *but* doesn't really count."

Another habit in everyday conversation and negotiation is the use of superlative, absolute, and judgmental descriptors: *always, never, very, should,* etc., which can actually shut down dialogue and erode trust because they imply that the speaker is set in their outlook and not open to another perspective. As a mediator, when I hear parties use these everyday and seemingly innocent words, it's my job to reframe the message in a way that keeps the recipient at the table:

From blame to problem-solving. "I can appreciate how you each believe the other person contributed to this miscommunication, and I have good news: we can use what happened there to formulate some strategies to prevent it from happening again."

From past to future. "If our rearview mirror was as big as our windshield, we'd never get anywhere. I've been listening to you both and have some ideas as to how we can look forward through that windshield, if you are open to hearing them."

From ultimatum to aspiration. "It sounds like what you're saying is that you have other suppliers who are interested in your business. From what I've heard, you'd like to maintain continuity with your current supplier, with modified terms."

From judgment to empathy. "When you say she's 'unreliable,' it sounds like punctuality is an important quality for you in a working relationship."

Often the language we use is a question of style. Even the act of interrupting is stylistic and can be viewed as either rude or encouraging depending on the conversational styles of the participants to the dialogue. Deborah Tannen is an American author and professor of linguistics at Georgetown University. She has written many books on conversational style, indirectness of language, and especially on gender differences in language. Her research has focused on how conversational expression impacts interpersonal relationships, and especially the interplay of what she calls "connection" and "power" maneuvers in family conversations.

Among other examples, Tannen mentions a wife who refuses to let her husband make popcorn by saying, "You always burn it." According to Tannen, the wife's resistance to her husband's request is a control maneuver, but by referencing a potential ill effect for her family (i.e., burnt popcorn), she ties a connection maneuver into her attempt to enforce a decision. A mediator might reframe the popcorn statement to, "It sounds like you enjoy popcorn cooked at different levels of done-ness." Then, she might get the parties to generate options: "What would happen if you made two batches?" or "What if you bought a small microwave for the garage where [husband] could make more well-done popcorn that wouldn't permeate the house with burned-popcorn aroma?"

The language used in family interactions, friendships, the workplace, dealmaking, and peacemaking can escalate or de-escalate a situation or even make or break relationships. You don't need to be a sociolinguist to pause and think about the language you use before speaking the words, especially when you need to make a deal. In the next chapter, we'll discuss how you can frame a question to solicit a *no* response to actually mean *yes*. You can also use *yes* to replace *no*.

For example, instead of:

> *Mommy, can I have some ice cream?*
>
> *No. You haven't eaten your peas.*

Try:

> *Yes, as soon as you eat your peas.*

You can also use language to create the appearance of a choice. This was always a parenting favorite of mine:

> *Would you like to take your bath before or after the movie?* (The bath is nonnegotiable.)

If you think, "That's so obvious, it would never work on intelligent adults," try it:

> *Do you [school] propose speech therapy as a service incorporated into the classroom or separate from the classroom for our son?* (The speech services are nonnegotiable.)

Mediators, in particular, are known for using certain "magic" words and phrases to keep the parties looking forward, discover hidden interests, generate options, and maintain an attitude of optimism. We also work with the parties' belief systems and points of resistance—their map of reality, not ours ("I get that this has been difficult. The goal now is to make things better").

We use prefatory language:

- Appreciating that . . .
- Understanding that . . .
- Recognizing that . . .
- Accepting/assuming that . . .

We fuel hope and creativity to break down barriers:

- Imagine if . . .
- I wonder what would happen . . .
- If money and time weren't obstacles . . .
- I'm hopeful that . . .

You don't have to be a mediator to sprinkle some magic language dust on your own negotiation!

The Language of Empathy

Through the ten years I taught negotiation and mediation to law students, empathy was a key skill I emphasized. It's powerful, humanizing, and you concede nothing by conveying it. I stand by that. But I don't have to. Turns out, it's scientific.

One of the sessions I attended at the February 2022 Neuroleadership Institute's summit unveiled the results of three years of research on a way to accurately think about, measure, and build empathy, based on critical stages in how we connect with and understand others. After so many years evangelizing its benefits, it was exciting to learn about a way to build empathy at scale in a science-based way. As David Rock, co-founder and executive director of the Neuroleadership Institute put it, "The past two years have taught us there's a stark disconnect between the values leaders are touting and what employees are actually experiencing—and that's led to the need for more compassionate executives. Compassion doesn't look the same for everyone." Jamil Zaki, professor of psychology at Stanford University, who spoke at the conference, also reinforced the perspective that empathy is a skill, and that "there is no choice between empathy and bottom-line success because they feed into each other."

⚡ Everyday Super Tip

Expressing empathy does not mean *agreeing* with what the other person is saying. That's what makes it so powerful in negotiation: it contributes to rapport and trust without requiring any concessions.

In an interview with *The New Yorker*, actor Alan Alda shared an anecdote from early in his career when working with director Mike Nichols on the Broadway musical, *The Apple Tree*. At one point during rehearsal, Nichols observed of Alda and his scene partner, "You're not relating to each other much at all. You kids think relating is the icing on the cake. It's the *cake*." From that point on, Alda practiced empathy as much as he could, describing it as a muscle. "If you build up that muscle, the floodgates open," Alda remarked. In that same interview Alda stated, simply and beautifully, "Listening is the best part of communicating." (chapter 5). Something tells me, Alan Alda is a superstar negotiator . . .

Preparing your negotiation plan; thinking about and preparing questions to explore the other party's BATNA, interests, and needs; and then truly listening to the other party are all opportunities to introduce empathy into everyday conversations and negotiations. The third step of the chapter 5 listening model, **reflecting back**, is your window for using language to demonstrate empathy:

- "I appreciate how hard this is for you."
- "That must have hurt your feelings."
- "I can tell you have a lot going on."
- "That sounds really challenging."
- "I get how you felt that was unfair."
- "I totally see why you would be embarrassed."
- "How exciting!"
- "I bet that took courage."

Simply put, empathy isn't just a "nice-to-have" skill. It's an everyday imperative in business and personal relationships, and displaying empathy can represent a pivotal moment in negotiation.

The Language of Apology

People sometimes think nonmonetary needs, interests, or demands in a negotiation or mediation can be an easy item to toss in because the other party doesn't have to cut a check. Not so. Nonmonetary aspects can, indeed, be the final detail that closes a deal—or holds one up because they implicate the other party's ego, effort, or time. It's easier for some people and organizations to throw in an extra $5,000.

Possibly the most common nonmonetary "ask" in negotiation and mediation is the apology. Sometimes starting off with an apology is the path to continuing to negotiate at all because that's just how important it is to that person. If an apology factors into your negotiation or settlement, there's a right way to do it. A sincere apology should include the following elements:

A statement of gratitude	"Thank you for talking to me about this / bringing this to my attention. If you hadn't done so, I wouldn't have realized it."
A statement of apology for specific behavior or actions	"I'm sorry that I criticized you in front of the group."
An explanation of why you behaved the way you did	"Usually, we do something different, and I was caught off guard."
An expression of remorse	"I feel terrible about this."
Acceptance of responsibility and offer to help / repair any damage	"It was rude / disrespectful / careless of me."
A request for forgiveness	"Can you forgive me?"
A promise regarding the future	"I won't let this happen again."

Do *not:*

Blame	"It's just that you always interrupt me in meetings" (there's that word *always*).
Make excuses	"I'm under a lot of pressure, you know."
Defend	"I didn't mean to cause offense."
Negate	"I'm sorry you feel that way / I'm sorry if you were offended."
Deflect	"If I did behave as described …"

Many find an in-person apology more impactful than a written apology, which can come across as detached and wordsmithed. For some, a (sincere!) written apology carries the day.

S. Lucia Kanter St. Amour, *It's the Cake*. Watercolor on paper.

CHAPTER 10

"ARE WE THERE YET?" THE USE OF QUESTIONS IN NEGOTIATION

I've already mentioned this: kids are natural negotiators. To name a few of their effective traits, they are motivated, curious, imaginative, persistent . . . and . . . inquisitive!

Kids—especially young kids—ask tons of questions:

- Where do bubbles go?
- Why don't we have tails?
- Are there more bricks in the world or feathers?
- Why can't we breathe underwater?
- What do you call the in-between spaces on a comb?
- How do I know I'm real and not just a dream of someone else?

The skillful use and timing of questions can be transformative in everyday interactions and negotiation. What's the purpose of questions?

- **To gather information:** needs, feelings, opinions, interests, past or current practice, available resources, etc.
- **To express curiosity:** to show interest in the other side, build rapport, genuinely connect.
- **To test assumptions:** ("We had assumed you wanted to source the work for this project locally. Is that correct, or are you willing to expand your search?")
- **To check understanding / get clarification** ("What do you mean when you say it will be a stretch to get approval?")
- **To get an opinion:** ("What did you think of some of our past designs on other projects that we sent for your review?")
- **To create an opportunity to listen and express empathy:** Suppose your counterpart has received three phone calls from complaining customers during the span of fifteen minutes. You might ask, "Are you having a tough day?"
- **To ask for help:** (see chapter 3. Getting "help" from the other side during the negotiation is also an effective tactic. People actually like to be asked to help!)

✐ Everyday Super Tip

Watch out for the *statement dressed up as a question*. Kids and spouses are particularly crafty with this: "Are we there yet?" "Are you going to just stand there with the refrigerator door open like that?" Those are not questions! Those are opportunities for reflecting back the emotion underneath the superficial words (see chapter on listening). "You're tired of being in the car, aren't you?" or "You seem agitated. What's on your mind?"

Now I'll pause for a quick note on gender disparity when it comes to questions (using cisgender vocabulary because that is the way the authors researched the subject): When Linda Babcock and Sara Laschever, co-authors of *Women Don't Ask: Negotiation and the Gender Divide,* wondered how come male graduate students were teaching their own courses while female students were always assigned as assistants, her dean said, "More men ask. The women just don't ask." Drawing on psychology, sociology, behavioral economics, and dozens of interviews with people in different disciplines and at all phases of their careers, *Women Don't Ask* explores how our institutions, child-rearing methods, and implicit assumptions dissuade women from asking for opportunities and resources——perpetuating a vicious cycle of inequality. *Women Don't Ask* coaches women how to ask and why they should.

Before we discuss the use of questions during a negotiation, we need to talk about questions to consider in advance of a negotiation. This harkens back to the chapter on planning. The first question to ask, consistent with Step 1 of planning, is **What is the problem I'm trying to solve?** This is not a question to be given cursory consideration. Sometimes you think you know what the *presenting* problem is (e.g., school absenteeism and how to reduce it—OK, time to talk solutions). Well, hold on. Is school absenteeism the problem or the manifestation of a *root* problem(s)? Dedicating time for research and extremely focused thinking on problem identification and definition can save you hours, even days, of work and negotiation time later on.

Alexandra Carter, author of *Ask for More,* walks through ten questions—five "Mirror" questions to ask yourself and five "Window" questions to ask the other party. The focus of Carter's book is on the *internal* negotiation with yourself and using certain key questions to increase your own awareness (see Step 10 of planning in chapter 2). The nuances of Carter's ten-question approach track the priorities of the superpower of everyday negotiation I impart here. Carter actually uses the school absenteeism example. After engaging in the process of asking investigative questions—which Carter aptly describes as "spending time to save time"—it turned out that the root problem in that school district wasn't lack of interest in learning, parents not prioritizing school, laziness, or even transportation—it was that the kids didn't have clean clothes and would stay home out of embarrassment. With this information, the school district partnered with local businesses to provide drop-off clothes-washing services at school sites, and the percentage of students attending school at least 90 percent of the time leaped from 46 percent to 84 percent.

There are two main types of questions:

1. **Closed-ended and restrictive.** These can be answered briefly with a yes or no. These are useful for securing a specific bit of information, directing a conversation to a desired area, or gaining commitment to a definite position, e.g., "You'll send the revised quotation by Monday night, right?" Closed-ended questions can be useful in parenting by offering the illusion of a choice, as mentioned previously: "Would you like peas or broccoli with your mac 'n cheese for dinner?" Closed-ended questions that can be answered with a one- or two-word response by the witness are the type used in cross-examination during a trial or a deposition where the inquisitor needs to retain

as much control as possible so that the respondent doesn't launch into a narrative.

2. **Open-ended and expansive.** These do not lead your counterpart in any specific direction. Generally speaking, open-ended questions reveal much more about objectives, needs, current situation, and behavioral style than restrictive questions. Example: "How do you feel about moving out of your home before the holidays?" or "You seem uneasy with my offer. Which aspects are the biggest obstacles?"

Five Keys to Proper Questioning

1. **Have a plan.** (Does this advice sound familiar?) Have a goal in mind. Ask yourself, "What type of information will help me make a good decision? Am I more likely to get that information by being direct or by disguising my questions?"

2. **Know your counterpart.** Also echoing chapter 3: the more you find out about your counterpart, the better you can target your questions.

3. **Move from the broad to the narrow.** As you gain information from answers to broad questions, start asking questions that yield more specific information. For example, if you ask someone selling a car, "Did you keep maintenance records?" and they say yes, you can proceed to ask about the type of records, the frequency of maintenance, etc.

4. **Use proper timing.** Be sensitive to your counterpart's feelings. If they find the questions offensive, they will provide less information and be less willing to negotiate. Example: asking someone how their diet is going while they eat a dessert is an example of poor timing.

5. **Ask permission to ask a question.** Remember my inquisition of the unsuspecting Girl Scouts from chapter 3? I asked permission first. Asking permission is polite, and it starts the swing toward agreement. Once you gain permission, your counterpart is more likely to give you a complete answer.

A Page From the Mediator's Playbook

Jim Melamed, founder and general counsel of mediate.com, explains in his online mediator certification course that a mediator asks between one hundred and five hundred questions in a mediation:

- **Nondirective opening** ("What's going on?")
- **Information gathering** (who, what, where, when, why)
- **Clarifying/specifying** ("What do you mean when you say ..." or "What would 'earning back trust' look like?")
- **Justifying** ("What's the motivation there?")
- **Stimulating** ("What other ways could this be done?" or "If the reverse were true, what would you do?")
- **Participation** ("Lucia, we haven't heard from you recently. What's going through your mind?")
- **Focusing** ("If we had to make a decision right now, what might that be?")

- **Alternate choice question** (the eye doctor question: "Which image is clearer—choice 1 or choice 2?")
- **Closure** ("I think we're there. The question now is, How can we best . . . ?")

Nothing prevents *you* from asking mediator questions of both yourself and the other party in a negotiation. Of all the questions a mediator asks, Melamed maintains that the **Outcome** question is probably the most important: "What would you like to accomplish? What results would you like to create? How do you want it to be? What are you looking for?" Follow that up with the **Evidence** question: "What would you need to experience to know that you had what you want?"

While you are engaged in the questioning process, remember to then use your listening skills! Pay close attention not only to what is being said but the emotion beneath the words, mannerisms, and gestures (see chapter 5). Also notice *what they aren't saying* and what they do and do not answer. There's a reason this book is ordered as it is, with listening before questioning. It's all part of the design! More than that, as I've learned from various hostage negotiators—who I would always invite to my law class for the questioning module—you can only broach questions after you've built rapport and trust, which we covered at the outset of this book.

One particular hostage negotiator I'd like to talk about—though he never visited my class—is Chris Voss. During the 2020 COVID shelter-in-place orders, when everything shut down and schools were closed and hadn't even begun to design remote learning—I mean when everything just plain stopped—my boys were a freshman and sophomore in high school. I wasn't going to let them sit around all day on YouTube or playing video games. Fortunately, I had the means to purchase a Masterclass.com subscription. I figured it was a fun way for the boys to pick their own "classes," as it were—and from celebrities they knew and liked (basketball skills from Steph Curry counted as P.E., Aaron Sorkin's screenwriting class counted as English composition, etc.).

I noticed a course on negotiation by none other than Chris Voss. If that name isn't familiar to you, I'll fill you in: he was a hostage negotiator with the FBI for thirty years and the author of a best-selling book, *Never Split the Difference*. This is an individual with life-or-death negotiating skills under serious pressure, with police blockades in place and sharpshooters waiting for the signal. Fun fact: Remember the "repeat their last one to three words" advice from chapter 5 as the training wheels for the reflecting back step of the listening loop? Chris Voss will tell you the same thing, and he calls it Mirroring. He recounts a story of a friend who confided in his wife before attending a party together one evening, that all he planned to do in conversations with other party guests the entire evening was apply Mirroring and Labeling techniques he had learned from Voss. By the end of the soiree, several people commented to his wife what a "fascinating" person her husband was!

I'll share two nuggets that really stuck with me from the class because they are directly on point with this chapter:

1. **"No-oriented" questions.** I was trained on the previously mentioned Roger Fisher & William Ury *Getting to Yes* and *Getting Past No* Harvard Program on Negotiation concept of, well, persuading people to say yes in

a negotiation. But Chris Voss turns this idea on its head, and his reasoning resonates. Trying to get someone to say yes is thorny: Is it a trick? Can you be trusted? It implies commitment or making promises, and they don't want to be pinned down. No wonder it's so hard to do!

Instead, our very clever Mr. Voss teaches the no-oriented question—that is, getting them to say no—which gently and naturally leads them to a yes. No is safe. No isn't a commitment. No leaves you options. For example, "Would it be totally unrealistic for you to get back to us in the next forty-eight hours with an answer?" or "Is it impossible to give us some wiggle room on price?" or "Would it be bothersome if I followed up next week?"

2. **Caution with using "WHY."** Echoed by Alexandra Carter, author of *Ask for More*, Voss says *WHY* puts people on the defensive. He uses the example of when you were a kid and broke something and were asked by an exasperated parent, "Why did you do that?" You had done something wrong. You had to defend yourself— and you couldn't. Instead—and this is where Voss's techniques dovetail so nicely with the mediator tool kit—you ask about HOW someone might make something happen, or WHAT makes it important to them: *What* does that do for you? *What* led you to that conclusion? *What* factors went into your decision? *How* would that work? *How* do you see that playing out? *Who* are some of the people that could help make that happen (or get in the way of that happening)? *Who* can help (or would need to be involved)? *When* do you need to know? *When* did you decide that?

In a recent conversation with a neighbor, she shared in some detail her husband's concern over transgender athletes in competition sports and, seeking confirmation for a particular value proposition, urged me, "I'm just worried that we're losing our traditional values in this country, aren't you?" "Noise" invaded my mind and then I heard that otherworldly voice from within me: "*Seek first to understand . . .*" (see chapter 5). Successfully reining my noise, and rather than asking "*Why* would you say that?," I queried her, "Well, I'm not sure I understand what you mean. *What do you mean* by 'traditional values'? Can you give some examples?" After citing to the decline in recitation of the Pledge of Allegiance in grade schools, she found herself a bit addled. She found, in fact, that she did not know what she meant. She had been parroting a phrase she'd heard as a refraining chorus from others—family members, selective media outlets— and had adopted wholesale. Politicians routinely employ this strategy—called "keyword squatting"—wherein they leverage their position of social authority (see Cialdini, chapter 13) and repeat a certain phrase to the point that it is widely accepted without further scrutiny. My neighbor then thanked me for "being curious enough to ask that question," and said that I had really given her something to think about.

Another hiccup with the "why" question is: people may not *know* why. That can be a tough question to answer. If you ask me why my favorite color is green, I might say, "I don't know! It's not a rational thing. I just like it." But if you ask me, "What is it about the color green that appeals to you?" or even "How do green hues make you feel?" I could say, "Oh! It reminds me of lying in the yard as a kid and looking up at the sky and smelling the grass, and it makes me feel relaxed and free; and it looks nice against the tone of my skin; or it reminds me of how content I feel when I observe the beauty of the endless verdant splendor of the trees, hills, and mountains around my home." Now we're getting somewhere.

⚡ Everyday Super Tip

My caution about the WHY question is a perspective—not an absolute or a prohibition. It doesn't always put someone on the defensive, and I don't profess absolutes. It can be a good empathy and curiosity question, as I used with Lily Din in episode 11 of the *Forces of Good: The Superpower of Everyday Negotiation* podcast: "What is Danceable and why did you start it?"

Earlier in the chapter 5, I suggested to you a *Super Stealth Question* ("Is there anything else?") and alluded to another *Super Stealth Question*. The wait is over. Here it is, as reinforced by Zoe Chance, professor at Yale School of Management (who also supports the power of the No-oriented question). I've deployed this one for many years. Chance calls it her Magic Question:

⚡ Super Stealth Question #2:

"What would it take?"

Here's the example Chance gave in an interview with NPR. In Zambia, there was a conference about sex trafficking where Gloria Steinem was an expert, talking on this issue and giving advice. She went to a village that was struggling with that problem. Three young women had been lost to sex traffickers the previous year. Instead of giving the people advice, she asked what would it take for that to never happen again. They said an electric fence. An electric fence? Yes. Evidently, when the corn reached a certain height, the elephants came, ate it, and trampled it. The people then had no food. They had nothing to sell at the market. No money to send their kids to school. And these women and their families were desperate and turned to sex trafficking. So Gloria Steinem returned home, raised a few thousand dollars, sent them the money. She returned to the village a few years later; there was a bumper crop of corn. No women had left the village to sex trafficking since they had gotten the fence. It was not that the fence magically prevented sex trafficking but that no one needed to leave the village for that reason.

But the Super Stealth Question isn't exclusive to a high-stakes situation. Chance also gives the example (and one that made me think she was a fly on the wall in my home) of your kid not putting clothes in the hamper. Ask, "What would it take for you to put the clothes in the hamper?" Ask your friends, "What would it take for us to go on a vacation together?" Whatever it is that you want, just start asking, "What would it take?" And you might be surprised by the epiphanies that surface—which circles us right back to that first question of asking yourself, "What's the problem I'm trying to solve?"

See? It's all connected!

For a demonstration of using questions, including this Super Stealth question, listen to episodes 12 and 13 of the *Forces of Good: The Superpower of Everyday Negotiation* podcast.

CHAPTER 11

STICK OR SNAKE? BASIC BRAIN SCIENCE IN NEGOTIATION

G rab your laboratory coat and chemistry set because this is the part where you get to dress up as a brainy neuroscientist! Consider this chapter a primer in neuroscience, emotions, and how they impact decision-making in negotiation, along with understanding the myth of rationality. Some of these "aha!" nuggets may have you recalling earlier scenarios in your own life and can help navigate difficult moments in everyday negotiation.

Disclaimer: I'm not a neuroscientist! I'm not even strong in the sciences (though I held my own in mathematics). So I'm confident that anyone who has made it this far in this book can gain a basic understanding of the crossover of neuroscience and negotiating.

The starting point is to recognize that people negotiating a problem or even a deal are in some state of arousal, discomfort or crisis. In such a state, the brain shops its handy inventory of hormones to secrete, a favorite of which is cortisol—the stress hormone. Cortisol levels impact:

- **Decision-making**
- **Risk assessment**
- **Rational cognition**
- **Focus**
- **Working memory** (how much information a person can hold, process, and use at any given moment)
- **Perception of threat**

The brain responds by and large the same way for both physical threats (a snake) and emotional threats ("She's going for full custody of the kids" or even "I just got outbid on eBay with only two minutes left in the auction"—also cue the adrenaline hormone). The *cognitive response* toggles between three fundamental levels of functioning: *reptilian* (fight or flight, the neural networks related to fear/survival—a very durable network); *paleo-mammalian* (social bonds, decisions); and *neocortical* (high-level executive functions).

The exercise of law, engineering, accounting, science, etc., is a neocortical activity, but decision-making is a sub-neocortical activity. So, when someone suddenly shifts position and we think they are acting "irrationally," a different part of the brain—the nonexecutive part—has taken over. Even the common act of getting angry at one's kids is a *core relational theme* (more on that below) left over from the reptilian brain: "My progeny is in danger, and I need to act." But if the executive/higher brain reappraises in time, it can ask whether anger is really the appropriate response to the situation.

The brain employs a three-goal system:

- **Avoid** (threats, penalty, pain—aka, sticks)
- **Approach** (rewards—aka, carrots)
- **Attach** to other people (human bonding)

Although we are wired to cooperate socially and to bond, we are very reactive to threats, and the brain has a **negativity bias**; this means the sympathetic nervous system lights up like a Christmas tree at even a whiff of a threat, and that "sticks" are more impactful than "carrots"!

This is where we need to talk about the amygdala-hippocampus system.

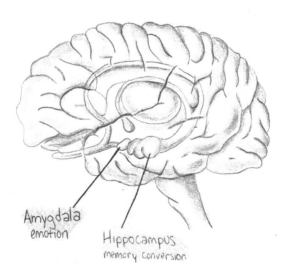

Katherine Lemke, *Amygdala-hippocampus system*.
Colored pencil on paper.

It is primed to label experiences negatively and will flag a negative experience prominently in the memory. With ambiguous communication or information, this means that *if* a negative inference can be made, it *will* be made, in lieu of a positive interpretation. That is, when in doubt, we will mistake the stick for a snake nine times out of ten to avoid the one time in ten that we mistake the snake for a stick!

The negativity bias is so sturdy that, as studied by the famous psychologist John Gottman, five positive interactions are required to overtake a single negative one (in the early 1990s, Gottman studied married couples talking for fifteen minutes about something innocuous and predicted with 94 percent accuracy traits that led to couples ending up divorced). Thus, people will do more to avoid a loss than realize a gain; and the *Avoid* system is routinely hijacking the *Approach* and *Attach* system. The result of threat reactivity is that parties in a dispute overestimate threat and underestimate opportunity in their initial appraisals. If you aren't able to recalibrate, to reappraise that the snake is a stick, the brain continues to pump cortisol and reinforce stress. The cost of not reappraising is that actions and decisions while feeling threatened lead to overreactions, which causes other people to feel threatened, and then you're caught in a vicious cycle. The *Approach* system is inhibited, thus limiting options and opportunities.

∕ Everyday Super Tip

Let go of the myth. Understand that it is more likely people will deviate from rationality than be consistently rational. Use active listening (chapter 5) and reframing, and recognize when it's time to take a break for the brain to reappraise and stop the vicious cycle.

A Word About the Role of Emotions

I'll share what I have learned from my thirty-plus hours of training in lie detection and emotional micro-expression from the Paul Ekman Group—an education and training organization founded by the very same Paul Ekman previously referenced—to teach skills for recognizing lies and emotions, as well as Ekman's book *Emotions Revealed: Core Relational Themes.* They inform how we deal with people in the world. Our *cell assemblies* have, over thousands of years, created a sturdy *emotion alert database.* This database serves an important purpose:

FEAR protects us; our lives are saved because we are able to respond to threats of harm protectively, without thought.

DISGUST reactions make us cautious about indulging in activities that literally or figuratively might be toxic.

SADNESS and despair over loss signals to others that we may need help.

Even **ANGER** is useful; it warns others, and us as well, when things are thwarting us.

Perhaps the juiciest nugget I learned from *Emotions Revealed* is the concept of the *refractory state.* This is the time during which our thinking cannot incorporate information that does not fit with the emotion we are feeling. For example, have you ever tried to apologize to someone while they are still mad at you? It's futile. A refractory state lasts an average of twenty minutes, and the person experiencing the strong emotion simply cannot take in any new information until the refractory state has passed.

Recognizing a refractory state (in yourself or someone else) can be key in terms of what you do or say next in everyday life or negotiation. Go ahead and write that scathing email reply . . . and save it for later review when the refractory state has passed (or ask someone else to review it). I don't even want to tell you how many emails I've written and *not* sent! When you identify the refractory state, understand that the executive level of the brain is not operating during this period—and it may be time for a break.

As a mediator, I have learned that rationality is a myth. Instead, human behavior and circumstances are *predictably irrational* (the title of another book I recommend, by Dan Ariely). Coming to grips with this reality can demystify how people (including you) behave in negotiation (and in life). Even as an attorney and mediator well trained in analytical reasoning, I now know better than to hail reasoned and analytical dialogue as the dominating mode to achieve settlement. Rational choice is just one approach to negotiation and conflict, and not necessarily the most effective one where emotions, distrust, and suspicions simply cannot be suspended even among people of goodwill and reason.

(P.S. Everyone believes they are a person "of good will and reason.")

More important than rationality is feeling *a sense of belonging*. According to social psychologist Mari Fitzduff, our "wars" today appeal to instincts and savage emotions, not rationality. They are about identity, inequality, and exclusions. We have feelings and instincts to serve our survival as human beings, through

1. environment;
2. hormones (cortisol, dopamine, serotonin, oxytocin, adrenaline, testosterone); and

3. DNA. In fact, Fitzduff discusses a gene variant called the DRD4-7R, which affects dopamine—people with it are more likely to be open-minded and to enjoy pleasure from variety, novelty, and diversity. fMRI scans show how variances in biology and genetics influence differences in attitudes and beliefs: Conservatives have larger amygdala structures (that is, the emotions/fear center of the brain) and higher startle responses than liberals; they are more likely to support capital punishment, stricter immigrant controls, and more military spending. People at the lower amygdala end are happier in general (and experience less startle response).

✐ Everyday Super Tip

Most people need to belong more than they need to be right. Chapter 2 imparted the importance of building rapport and connecting with people. Now you understand it's also scientific!

Brains differ on a continuum in responding to new information, uncertainty, fear, and strangers. Biologically, humans have evolved to be cooperative—but only with some people! This point dovetails with in-group versus out-group dynamics that cause us to reject and discredit people who are not "insiders" in our group or belief system, and credit too generously, without objective evaluation, those who are members of our group. Testosterone and oxytocin (the same hormones that ancient warriors produced) increase a sense of belonging and reduce fear. They also promote ethnocentric behavior and increase suspicion and rejection of others outside the tribe. As Fitzduff puts it, "Oxytocin binds us, but also blinds us." The need to belong is a major driver of war.

When beliefs are contradicted, fMRI showed an increase in emotion (amygdala response) but no increase in cortex reasoning. When people are in conflict, they like things to be simple, and it is more likely that nuanced categories of people get hurt (because they are confusing).

Don't overcomplicate things. Slow down. Simplify. Remember my advice from chapter 2: *Make it easy for them.*

A closing comment about neuroscience, fMRI scans, and scientific jargon in general: Even as someone who cites brain science consistently, I bristle at how fashionable this has become in the mainstream media and how often it's tossed into TED Talks by those with no background or training in science. Scientific lingo is one of the best ways to sell ideas. For example, the word *halitosis* was almost completely unknown to the public at large until the early twentieth century when businessman Gerard Lambert parlayed it to sell a new product called Listerine. By giving a banal fact of life (bad breath) a scientific-sounding label, Lambert dramatically augmented the authority and desirability of his product.

The media loves to cover new fMRI results, and the business world is hungry for the consumer brain to be decoded. Unfortunately, studies are often tiny because of the high costs of running the machine and interpreting the results, and the data can be tough to interpret. Some years ago, a study of a salmon, for instance, showed the "fish's brain exhibited increased activity for emotional images."

The only problem? The fish was dead. In fairness, the technology has improved since then!

S. Lucia Kanter St. Amour, *Resonant Koi in Rainbow Seaweed.*
Watercolor and distressed ink on paper.

CHAPTER 12

BIGSHOT vs. WALLFLOWER: NEGOTIATION STYLE AND BEHAVIOR

If I asked what your negotiating *style* is, what would you say? And I don't mean breezy beach flip-flop versus minimalist vegan-leather loafer. A critical competency for today's professionals—and one that will give you that added edge in your everyday negotiations in any context, professional or personal—is to understand that we each have our own way of dealing with conflict. Conflict is normal—healthy even. It's an opportunity for growth and change that may be overdue. It's a common part of any workplace, community, or family. Unfortunately, it can also lead to heartache, lost productivity, and mental health issues. At the same time, conflict can be a motivator that generates new ideas and innovation, and a better understanding of relationships and organizational practices. Converting conflict into success means effective management. At both University of California law schools at Berkeley and San Francisco, we taught the Thomas-Kilmann Conflict Mode Instrument (TKI) to gain insight into the various conflict styles—or *modes*. The TKI is the world's most-used conflict management tool for the workplace.

The TKI begins by identifying the two basic dimensions of conflict behavior:

- **Assertiveness** is the degree to which you try to satisfy your own concerns during a conflict. This is related to how you might try to meet your needs or receive support for your ideas.

- **Cooperativeness** is the degree to which you try to satisfy the other individuals. It is related to how you might try to help the other individual meet his or her needs or how you can be receptive to the other individuals' ideas.

The TKI assessment applies these to the five conflict-handling **modes** listed below. By applying the basic two dimensions of Assertiveness and Cooperativeness to the five conflict-handling modes, you create the five major combinations possible in a conflict situation.

- **Competing** is assertive and uncooperative. In this mode, you try to satisfy your own concerns at the other person's expense.

- **Collaborating** is both assertive and cooperative. In this mode, you try to find a win-win solution that completely satisfies the concerns of both individuals involved.

- **Compromising** is intermediate in both assertiveness and cooperativeness. In this mode, you try to find an acceptable solution that only partially satisfies both individuals' concerns.

- **Avoiding** is both unassertive and uncooperative. In this mode, you work to sidestep the conflict without attempting to satisfy either individual's concerns.

- **Accommodating** is unassertive and cooperative. In this mode, you try to satisfy the other person's concerns at the expense of your own concerns.

So which mode is best? All of them! All modes are useful and effective, depending on the context and the conflict style of the other party. I recall how some of my law students were disappointed to test as dominant in Avoiding because they perceived it as "weak." But imagine, for example, just how effectively an individual with an Avoiding style might thwart a counterpart with a Competing style, causing the Competing individual to become impatient and make concessions so they can get a deal.

There is no single best way to handle every conflict. Each of the five conflict-handling modes has its own set of benefits and costs. Each can be highly effective if used properly in the right circumstance. To be a truly effective negotiator, you will be familiar with your own natural conflict mode and learn the flexibility to adopt other modes to suit a situation—while always remaining true to yourself. Importantly, you can learn to spot which mode comes naturally to the other party in your negotiation and understand strategies for being more persuasive with them.

S. Lucia Kanter St. Amour, *Negotiating Style.*
Watercolor and colored pencil on paper.

Now think back on the 1998 Russia hostage crisis. Which mode did my parents and I adopt? And was that the same mode that comes to me naturally in everyday interactions and negotiations when left to my own devices? Hint: my own TKI mode is co-dominant in Collaborating and Competing.

The TKI was pioneering in helping people in organizations analyze the way they think about conflict in terms of *style*—which represents a combination of behavior, personality, and motivation that can be difficult to change in a lasting way (though temporarily adopted to fit the circumstances, as I have suggested). But what about *behavior*? Coaches all over the world turn to the Conflict Dynamics Profile (CDP) as a tool to zero in on conflict behaviors—which is especially useful information to individuals whose goal is to change. The CDP highlights the following fifteen behaviors (as well as nine "Hot Buttons"):

Constructive Behaviors	Destructive Behaviors	"Hot Buttons"
Active Constructive Perspective Taking Creating Solutions Expressing Emotions Reaching Out	**Active Destructive** Winning at All Costs Displaying Anger Demeaning Others Retaliating	Unreliable Overly Analytical Unappreciative Aloof Micromanaging Self-Centered Abrasive Untrustworthy Hostile
Passive Constructive Reflective Thinking Delay Responding Adapting	**Passive Destructive** Avoiding Yielding Hiding Emotions Self-Criticizing	

The starting point for the CDP is a triggering event—something that sets the stage for conflict. It could be anything: a single upsetting behavior by another person (like burning the popcorn), a long-standing series of issues between people ("You always interrupt me"), a difference of opinion ("How can you believe critical race theory shouldn't be taught in schools?"), etc. The event can be anything that places the interests of individuals in opposition to one another.

The event sets into motion the dynamics of conflict, but the outcome of that process is yet to be determined. One of the biggest influences on how things unfold will be how people behave in the conflict. Are they focused on problem-solving or on personalities? Constructive responses minimize the conflict from developing further. They tend to reduce the tension and keep the conflict focused on ideas rather than personalities. Destructive responses, on the other hand, tend to escalate things and to focus on personalities.

Then the CDP evaluates how active or passive the responses are. With active responses the individual is proactive to the conflict or provocation; this can be either constructive or destructive. Passive responses, in contrast, do not require much in the way of an overt act from the person. In fact, they typically involve the person exercising restraint. Again, passive responses can be either constructive or destructive; that is, they can make things better or they can make things worse. Given, then, that behaviors can be either constructive or destructive, and either active or passive, responses to conflict on the CDP fall into one of four categories: Active-Constructive, Passive-Constructive, Active-Destructive, and Passive-Destructive.

Behavioral responses to provocation, which can determine whether the potential conflict is viewed through either the task-focused or person-focused lens, can also play a role later in the conflict sequence. For example, a situation can begin as a task-focused conflict centered on some non-personal issue with manageable levels of arousal, but destructive responses during this phase could shift and lead to a person-focused conflict instead. Alternatively, a dispute that started out focused on personalities could be "reined in" by careful behavioral work and evolve into a less destructive task-focused conflict.

Identifying Hot Buttons—the kinds of people or behaviors that are especially likely to trigger you—is another important feature of the CDP. When pushed, Hot Buttons can "poke the bear" (provoke conflict). The "hottest" Hot Buttons (that is, those that are most upsetting) will be the ones most likely to provoke a quick and automatic set of destructive responses (think refractory state from chapter 11), while the "cooler" Buttons are more likely to conjure a blend that includes some constructive behaviors. By understanding and examining the links between provocation and response, it becomes easier to control one's behavior. This connects back to the final Personal Reflection step of chapter 3 and planning.

✎ Everyday Super Tip

You do you! Ultimately YOU are the only person you can control in a negotiation or conversation. Investing some time in understanding your own conflict mode and style can be a powerful tool when in the throes of negotiation, as well as enabling you to "read" the other party's mode and style so that you can be agile and calibrate your approach.

CHAPTER 13

SENTIMENTAL COFFEE MUG: MENTAL MAPS AND TRAPS IN NEGOTIATION

Now we're really getting to icing on the cake—and at this point you've earned it! For decades, cognitive psychologists have researched how the brain processes information and what that produces in the outside world in terms of behavior. In the 1970s, two psychologists from Stanford University, Daniel Kahneman and Amos Tversky, started to study aspects of decision-making: Does the rational person actually make decisions based on innate cost-benefit economic analysis? Their work, which they called "prospect theory," created a new discipline of science known as behavioral economics, which earned them the Nobel Prize in economics in 2002. (Tversky had died by then, so technically the prize only went to Kahneman at the time it was bestowed. Kahneman has since become a living legend!)

According to behavioral economics, the rational person theory doesn't take into account all the reasons people behave the way they do. People make decisions relative to a reference point, and that reference point is the *status quo*—"where I am now."

Kahneman and Tversky categorized their work into a set of common heuristics: maps of shortcuts that the brain takes so that it can make decisions and function without causing us to collapse in fast-moving everyday life, which otherwise bombards us with far too much information to process. But many of these heuristics can also act as traps in a negotiation, if you aren't aware of them.

Let's look at a few of the most common mental maps and traps:

Confirmation bias is the tendency to search for or interpret information in the way that confirms one's preexisting beliefs, leading to statistical (and strategic) errors. When people would like a certain idea to be true, they end up believing it to be true. Confirmation bias is particularly problematic because it does not allow a person's perspective to change, even based on evidence. It enables people with opposing beliefs to dig their heels in further rather than to adapt their mindset to the surroundings.

Consider a person in a workplace personality conflict. Rather than talking to those people who might disabuse them of their negative impressions of the coworker, they usually gripe to people most likely to agree with them. As a result, their negative impressions become amplified in an echo chamber of agreement. The chorus they hear is, "Wow, she is awful to treat you that way." The complainer's blamelessness rises, while the image of the adversary is demoted further into someone really unsavory.

An attorney preparing for a trial will certainly conduct research into case law that supports their theory of the case so that they can persuade a judge or jury, but they will be committing a risky error if they only notice examples that conform to their theory of the case. There's a special and daunting word for when attorneys make mistakes—*malpractice*. So it's critical that the attorney also research cases that challenge their theory of the case so that they can prepare rebuttals and avoid being caught off guard.

This is yet another area where the art of negotiation meets science. Astrophysicist Neil deGrasse Tyson tells us the same thing: question your hypothesis. More important than proving it right, try every possible way to prove it wrong before deciding it's right.

⤤ Everyday Super Tip

Argue with yourself: to counteract confirmation bias, when preparing for a negotiation or even a difficult conversation, actively seek out information that contradicts your point of view.

Related to confirmation bias is the **overconfidence effect**. This is when we systematically overestimate our knowledge and our ability to predict. Overconfidence measures the difference between what people really know and what they think they know (it turns out the experts suffer even more from the overconfidence effect than laypeople do). Studies have found that over 90 percent of U.S. drivers rate themselves above average, 68 percent of professors consider themselves in the top 25 percent for teaching ability, and 84 percent of Frenchmen believe they are above-average lovers.

Reactive devaluation bias occurs when a proposal, business or otherwise, is devalued or seen negatively because it seems to originate from a negative or antagonistic source. For instance, a plan or idea is proposed by another employee with whom you've disagreed in the past. Consider the human resources professional who regularly receives complaints from the same employee;

we'll call him Carl the Complainer. Carl complains about the temperature in the office, that someone heated up a fish sandwich in the microwave break room that filled the room with fish odor, and that the copy machine paper isn't recycled. When Carl presents the HR representative with a complaint of workplace harassment, reactive devaluation can be a perilous (and illegal) cognitive trap if the HR associate doesn't make sure to separate the complaint from her overall impression of Carl as a petty "complainer."

In a mediation setting, I've witnessed reactive devaluation of a proposal suggested by opposing counsel or the other party. They may dismiss the proposal or offer out of hand, thinking, "If this is such a good deal for us, they wouldn't be offering it." This is an instance where taking some time to evaluate proposals objectively can pay off, or me presenting it to the other party as a "mediator's proposal" might be appropriate.

Reactive devaluation is also related to the brain's negativity bias and rejection of those who are not part of our "in-group"—that is, those whom our brain negatively appraises as not "belonging" (see chapter 11). It is a particularly insidious heuristic that can blind us in everyday situations and cause us to ignore important information and warnings. Reactive devaluation is nothing new and can be traced back to Greek mythology and Cassandra, the daughter of Priam, the king of Troy. Cassandra often predicted the future accurately but because she had a reputation for being "cursed," spoke in the cryptic language of oracles rather than plain language and simply asked too much of those around her in the way of challenging their beliefs and the status quo (see confirmation bias above), her warnings were routinely disbelieved.

"Cassandra Syndrome" is still a metaphor applied today in the contexts of politics, the environment, the corporate world, science, and psychology.

Reciprocity effect is extremely alluring, and one of the most powerful maps and traps. It's very simple: if someone does something for you, you'll naturally want to do something for them. When you offer something for free, people feel a sense of indebtedness toward you. For example, researchers tested how reciprocity can increase restaurant tipping. Tips went up 3 percent when diners were given an after-dinner mint. Tips went up 20 percent if, while delivering the mint, the waiter paused, looked the customers in the eye, and then gave them a second mint while telling them the mint was especially for them. In another study, 11 percent of people were willing to donate an amount worth one day's salary when they were given a small gift of candy while being asked for a donation, compared to 5 percent of those that were just asked for the donation. Think of a recent invitation to a friend's house for dinner where your friend insists that you need not bring anything other than yourself; it's almost impossible to just show up at the door empty-handed without bearing some contribution, such as a bottle of wine.

⫻ Everyday Super Tip

People enjoy the feeling of a "hard won" deal. Remember chapter 3 on planning and preparing your concessions? If you "give" a little, you are more likely to get concessions from the other side because the reciprocity effect is almost impossible to resist. It also helps everyone (including you) feel that the final deal was "hard won." I've said that three times now, so I must mean it.

Endowment effect. Once people own something—or have a feeling of ownership—they irrationally overvalue it, regardless of its objective market value. People feel the pain of loss twice as strongly as they feel pleasure at an equal gain, and they fall in love with what they already have and prepare to pay more to retain it. For example, in another Kahneman study, scientists randomly divided participants into buyers and sellers and gave the sellers coffee mugs as gifts. Then they asked the sellers for how much they would sell the mug and asked the buyers for how much they would buy it. Results showed that the sellers placed a significantly higher value on the mugs than the buyers did.

A variation of the endowment effect is the IKEA effect: a cognitive bias in which people place a disproportionately high value on products they partially created. For example, in one study, participants who built a simple IKEA storage box themselves were willing to pay much more for the box than a group of participants who merely inspected a fully built box.

If you are negotiating, for example, a sale/purchase negotiation, recognize that it may be difficult for the seller to objectively assess offers that fall below *their* personalized value of a beloved vintage car, the house where they brought home their first baby, etc.

⚡ Everyday Super Tip

Recognize that you, too, may have sentimental attachments to objects great and small, and this can cloud your judgment and lead to impasse in a negotiation over the objective value of the item. If you see this happening with the other party, try the powerful tool of empathy and give them some time to come to terms with separating from that item.

S. Lucia Kanter St. Amour, *Sentimental Coffee Mug*. Watercolor on paper.

Social proof. No matter how unique we think we are, we all have some degree of inherent desire to conform, to belong, to be accepted. Largely considered the go-to source on the psychology of persuasion, Robert Cialdini includes social proof as one that makes the top six of the psychology of influence. Consistency, reciprocity, the "liking" principle, authority, and scarcity (which we've already discussed) are the five others. Consider something as vapid and unnoticeable as TV show laugh tracks—they cue the viewer when something is supposed to be funny. People will more likely participate or comply when they see other people also doing something. Social proof is especially effective in situations of uncertainty, where the only source of information in the moment is to look to others for cues on what to do.

And while useful, social proof can also serve as a trap—even be dangerous. The 1978 Jonestown Massacre is one of the most terrifying examples of the underbelly of social proof. This was the

1978 mass-murder/suicide of members of the Peoples Temple cult at the behest of their charismatic but paranoid leader, Jim Jones, in the Jonestown agricultural commune in Guyana. Jones enacted his "revolutionary suicide" plan at the compound, which members had "practiced" in the past, in which a fruit drink was laced with cyanide, tranquilizers, and sedatives. The death toll exceeded nine hundred, including some three hundred children. This is where the cautionary phrase, "Drinking the Kool-Aid" originates—referring to the dangers of blind obedience or loyalty to a cause.

Perhaps you have heard of the famous study by social psychologists Stanley Milgram, Leonard Bickman, and Lawrence Berkowitz. They installed a man on a busy sidewalk in New York City. His only job was to stop and look upward for a minute. When just one man gazed at the sky, 4 percent of passersby also looked up. When the experiment was repeated with five men looking upward, 18 percent of passersby imitated the same behavior, and for fifteen men with upward craned necks, 40 percent followed suit.

Another study cited by Cialdini concerned charitable donations: showing people a list of their neighbors who had donated to a charity led to a substantial increase in funds raised. The more names on the list, the more people donated. Social proof is a basic arrow in a marketer's quiver. Consider "likes" in social media, Yelp reviews, customer product reviews, the use of influencers using a particular product or frequenting a particular restaurant or club . . . consider even that the fact that you've seen a queue of people waiting for entry to a club could be staged to create the impression it's a desirable place to be. The ploy is effective.

Cialdini explains:

> The greater the number of people who find any idea correct, the more the idea will be correct. . . . We will use the actions of others to decide on proper behavior for ourselves, especially when we view those others as similar to ourselves. . . . When we are uncertain, we are willing to place an enormous amount of trust in the collective knowledge of the crowd. . . . We seem to assume that if a lot of people are doing the same thing, they must know something we don't.

⚡ Everyday Super Tip

Remember chapter 10 on questions and gathering information, particularly in an unfamiliar context? Be that curious child. If pressured by social proof—e.g., everyone else is jumping from the cliff, why don't you?—get more information. Ask, "Well, how high is the cliff? Could I slide down it?"

CHAPTER 14

TIME-OUT ON THE FIELD: IMPASSE AND MEDIATION

MAN IN BLACK: Let me explain

VIZZINI: There's nothing to explain. You're trying to kidnap what I've rightfully stolen.

MAN IN BLACK: Perhaps an arrangement can be reached?

VIZZINI: There will be no arrangement [as Man In Black cautiously approaches] . . . And you're killing her.

MAN IN BLACK: Well, if there can be no arrangement, then we are at an impasse.

VIZZINI: I'm afraid so.

— *The Princess Bride,* Buttercup Films Ltd., 1987

Negotiation, while fun (have I convinced you yet?), is an effort. It takes preparation, time, and patience, which is in short supply in our instantaneous society of the internet, smartphones, and social media reactions. A tense moment, or feeling like you and the other party are "too far apart to ever agree," is not impasse. That's a natural part of the negotiation process. If you didn't take time to establish rapport, to listen, to exchange information, to ask questions, to explore interests, you're probably not at impasse. You can get over it!

True impasse happens when you've been working for some time on potential options to reach a deal or for resolution of the identified issues to a conflict and you have run out of road to travel. The wellspring of options and ideas by people of sound minds and good intentions has run dry and you are really stuck.

The first step in breaking through impasse echoes one of the first steps in planning for a negotiation in the first place: **identifying the problem**. Understanding the source of impasse increases your chances of breaking through it. Is it a lack of resources, authority, or asymmetry in power? Is there some structural or procedural obstacle preventing you from making progress? Is one party more emotional or risk-averse than the other? If you are unable to identify why you've reached impasse from a rational perspective, chances are that emotions—which we mediators treat as another category of facts—are the source.

This might be a good time to pause and evaluate what **mental maps and traps** or unresolved personal history could be in play: loss of face, endowment effect, desire to "win" (recall the chocolate negotiations), fear of changing the status quo, suspicion of being "tricked," hostility, ego, worry about the approval or reaction of a third-party audience.

While there's no magic formula for breaking impasse, explore ways to change the dynamic of the negotiation. Chances are, you won't stay stuck (recall the cat in the tree from chapter 6). It's just math, according to John Forbes Nash Jr.: "In multivariable calculus, there's often a number of solutions for any given problem." Do you need to redefine the problem, revisit the agenda, get other people involved? Do you need to conduct further research and gather additional information? Has leverage shifted or you miscalculated your own or the other side's BATNA or WATNA? Perhaps you are at impasse on one issue and you can leave it alone while you turn to other issues on the agenda. Do you need to grab a giant paper clip and a whiteboard and start a no-holds-barred brainstorming session? Do you need to go out and share a pizza? Group "breaking of bread" promotes oxytocin, the bonding hormone.

And what about that story (chapter 8) I advised you to keep in your negotiation tool kit to ease tense moments and dislodge impasse?

Or maybe you just need some peace and quiet or to take a walk outside. Plenty of research supports the benefits of the walking meeting for helping people bond and generate ideas.

⋀ Everyday Super Tip

Take your negotiation for a walk! Chemicals produced by the brain during an outdoor walk help break down barriers and promote cognition and creative thinking.

At impasse moments, it can also be beneficial to review what progress has been made and focus on the positive aspects of the negotiation process so far. Remaining optimistic, while difficult at times, is incredibly important in negotiation.

Threatening to walk away is also tempting. Here's my basic advice about threats: Don't make idle ones; if you do it, know that you will act on it. If none of these strategies works, there's still plenty of hope, and it may be time to call in reinforcements . . .

An experienced mediator.

Katherine Lemke, *Mediation Miracle*. Ink drawing.

So, you've already tried to work it out on your own without a satisfying result and have reached true impasse. Working with a competent mediator is *very* different from parties negotiating on their own. For one thing, each party is likely to behave differently with a mediator in the mix than when negotiating directly with one another. Mediators work with whatever you bring to us, without judgment, without imposing our will, and with skills including empathy, listening, and perspective-shifting. Assuming basic trust in the mediator, people also tend to share more feelings, facts, and other insights with a mediator that may have remained guarded in direct negotiation. Mediators are in the human complexity business. While mediation cannot guarantee specific results, mediation generally promotes:

Economical and rapid agreements. It takes at least a year to get a court date, and multiple years if a case is appealed. The mediation alternative often provides a timelier way of resolving disputes. When parties want to get on with business or their lives, mediation may produce more desirable and rapid results.

Mutually satisfactory outcomes and high rate of compliance. Parties are generally more satisfied with solutions that have been mutually agreed upon, as opposed to solutions that are imposed by a third-party decision-maker such as an arbitrator or a judge. In fact, mediated agreements are honored with about a 90 percent compliance rate because people are more likely to follow through and comply with their own nuanced terms than those imposed by a third-party decision-maker. Parties who mediate their differences are able to attend to the fine details of implementation. Negotiated or mediated agreements can include specially tailored procedures for how the decisions will be carried out, which enhances the likelihood that parties will actually comply with the terms of the deal.

Comprehensive and customized agreements. Mediated settlements are able to address both legal and extralegal issues. Mediated agreements often cover procedural and psychological issues that are not necessarily susceptible to legal determination. The parties can tailor their settlement to their particular situation. In a court of law, only the *legally relevant* facts and legal theories according to the rules of evidence will be considered in determining an outcome. You may not have the opportunity to tell your whole story or communicate what is important to you. In mediation, everything is relevant. Mediated negotiations that take into account the underlying interests of the parties can result in outcomes that are more satisfying than simple compromise decisions just to get things over with.

Personal empowerment. Mediation is a very powerful place to be because *you still retain full control*. Once you abandon negotiation and mediation in favor of an arbitration or court tribunal, you are yielding most of your control to your attorney and to an arbitrator or judge (or jury). *People who negotiate their own settlements often feel more powerful and can experience more of a cathartic sense of closure that truly allows them to move on with life.*

Confidentiality and open exchange of information. The open and free exchange of information facilitates the parties' ability to negotiate with each other in confidence. Both parties are working with the same base of information, so the process of reaching a resolution that makes sense to both is more efficient. The open and free exchange of information is protected both by law and by the confidentiality agreement that the parties and the mediator sign at the outset of the mediation. This means that the mediator cannot be called as a witness at a later trial, and neither party may divulge offers that were made through the course of the mediation. Also, when a mediator conducts private caucusing with each party, the parties can share information with her and ask her to only share certain information with the other side but keep other bits of information confidential. In other words, the mediator can gather more information from the parties than the parties may have been willing to share with each other when negotiating on their own (which may have been the source of impasse).

The law is one of many standards and options. Most parties want to be educated about the law. Many mediators try to strike a balance between their prediction of what a court would do and other "reality checking" standards. The law is just one of many standards that a mediator can use to facilitate an outcome that all parties feel is fair, efficient, wise, and durable. The law is more subjective than most people experience, and lawyers often disagree about what the law is, as do judges. Ideally, the law is just one ingredient in a mix of things that are relevant in mediation, along with other criteria.

The mediator is impartial but not neutral. (What?) An experienced mediator doesn't give advice to either party independently and can't act as a lawyer for either party. The mediator's role is to help parties come up with an agreement that they can all live with; to do that, the mediator makes a point of looking at the issues from all angles and can help the parties with perspective-shifting (see chapter 6)._

A basic tenet of mediators is impartiality. Some mediators describe themselves as neutral. Not to nitpick (but I will), but impartiality is not the same as neutrality. What's the difference? Impartiality means that mediators can give lots of information to the clients we work with, without giving direct advice to either side. Impartiality drives the process of negotiation forward, always ensuring fairness and evenhandedness—for example, ensuring that both people get the opportunity to speak or reflect on options under consideration as per the case—and without taking sides.

But we are not neutral. Neutrality implies a state of dispassion or indifference in the people or the process. As a mediator, I am highly interested and engaged at all steps of the process. An elite Bugatti racing car equipped with 1,500 horsepower will perform none of that power with the engine in neutral. ***We are always in gear***, actively involved in a number of tasks at any given moment—even if it appears as if we are doing "nothing."

If the parties reach a deal in mediation and think, "The mediator didn't seem to really do anything," I've done my job well. That, my friends, is the superpower of mediation.

I call this next watercolor *Plato's Tree*. It is inspired by a specific tree that I pass on my daily trail hike with my chocolate Labrador, and whenever I show it to someone else, they say, "Oh! That's the tree . . ." and they tell me about a particular in their own life. Hence "Plato's Tree": the tree Ideal. A mediator *meets the parties where they are*. If you see in *Plato's Tree* one from a childhood home or the park where you take your kids, a mediator will meet you in that state of mind. Mediation, like this tree, can be individualized. We don't get many "ideal" solutions in life. Yet your "ideal" solution to a conflict/problem/prospective business deal stands a better chance of manifestation in the mediation forum than it does when you hand off your autonomy and power to the traditional court system. And how does this tree make you feel? Because emotions are treated as another category of facts in a mediation.

I don't paint a tree without including the underground roots, the source of life and stability. A successful negotiation requires exploring interests and needs at the root of demands and positions— as well as generating options (check out the multicolored leaves) to meet those needs and interests. It requires curiosity about the other party to understand what they need, too. Climb this tree and look around, look up, look down . . . to gain a new perspective on problem-solving. A mediator is specially trained and practiced in all these skills. Finally, notice how a couple of branches gracefully extend toward the ground, allowing easy access for climbing. A mediator fosters a genuine sense of *belonging* for all participants, and we've discussed how not belonging is often a major driver of conflict. Everyone is invited—no secret treehouse password required!

Even if you still don't finalize a deal or settlement in mediation, chances are progress was made in that process. The situation is not a lost cause. A mediator doesn't lose hope!

S. Lucia Kanter St. Amour, *Plato's Tree.* Watercolor on paper.

CHAPTER 15

"HAND OVER YOUR MILK MONEY": NEGOTIATING WITH BULLIES

I'm not a fan of labeling someone a "bully" or any other moniker that is reductive and dehumanizing. People are multitudes, and I imagine those who exhibit bullying-type behaviors experience a fair amount of inner turmoil from which they cannot free themselves. Then again, when one displays a consistent pattern of abusive conduct, after being given the benefit of the doubt for one too many "bad hair" days, the cap toe oxford fits. I wish I didn't have as much experience with bullies as I do. I've dealt with bullies from time to time since grade school and as recently as a harrowing group bullying experience in a professional setting in 2021 that took me by surprise.

So you'd think I'd be a pro at handling bullies. Yet this was the most difficult chapter to write for one reason, and I'm sorry to be the one to break it to you . . .

I'm not convinced you *can* negotiate with bullies.

At least not alone.

In grade school when I was growing up, Troy was your stereotypical bully. He literally pinned kids against the wall and demanded our milk money. Each day at lunchtime, we'd line up outside the cafeteria to collect our single-serving public-school-subsidized carton of milk. It was three cents. My mom kept a dish of pennies in a drawer in the kitchen so that when my brother and I packed our lunches for school, we could grab three pennies from the dish to stash in a sandwich baggie and toss into our, respectively, *Planet of the Apes* and *Muppets* lunch boxes. I still remember my mom habitually asking, "Do you have your milk money?" She knew we did, but she couldn't help saying it. (Recall chapter 10. It was a statement dressed up as a question: "I'm your mother who loves you, and I can't help but check that you are well nourished in my absence.") What she didn't know is that I would routinely pack *two* sandwich baggies in my lunch box, each containing three cents. One never knew who Troy would single out for milk money. (It wasn't that he didn't have his own milk money. His family had substantial means. He seemed to harbor a sadistic need to terrorize others.) So my strategy was to navigate the path of least resistance and, if I was Troy's chosen one on a particular day, surrender some milk money—just not *my* milk money.

Troy's bullying persisted through middle school and worsened, particularly with me it seemed, though it has occurred to me since childhood that he didn't single me out and was an equal opportunity bully. My strategy with bullies as an adult—and looking back on Troy now—is to start with an attitude of empathy and compassion. I suspect that people who bully others are actually in a great deal of pain themselves. I imagine it must be difficult to live inside their heart and mind. But I admit my empathy has limits, and with the exception of Troy, I have stood up to every single bully since eighth grade. It hasn't gone very well for me. In each case, I hold my ground, but ultimately I am the one who has to walk away from the situation. Twice it has been a job; another time it was a community that I loved. Each time, it has hurt me deeply and taken quite a bit of time to heal.

In 2018 I traveled back to that small town in Illinois for the first time in thirty years (once I departed my bucolic surroundings for so-called greater pursuits in life, e.g., to attend college at UC Berkeley in 1988, my parents moved away, and I had not looked back). I returned for my thirtieth high school reunion, and many things about the town were just about the same, in the best way possible. The night of the main reunion event and dinner, I spotted Troy from across the pub where we had all gathered. I walked over to the bar and eavesdropped on him for a while. "Maybe he grew out of it and is a good guy now," I mused. After all, no one gets a free pass through adolescence, which could have been particularly difficult for him due to factors unknown to the outside world.

Nope. As I listened to the vituperative tone and crass language he sputtered with his compadres at the bar, he was the same Troy. When I returned home, I looked him up on LinkedIn and saw that he was a C-level executive working in . . . wait for it . . . human resources.

Bullies succeed in the world. Bullies win. Bullies don't give up until you aren't just defeated, you are crushed. When I think about some of the "greatest" innovators in the history of the technology industry just down the road from me in Silicon Valley, for example, many of them have been classic bullies.

One aspect that makes them so effective is that they don't bluff. While bluffing can have a place in everyday negotiation, it's risky and one needs to consider context and stakes. When a bully threatens an action or consequence, they follow through. And so should you. This is one aspect of bullying behavior that is legitimate in more responsible hands (those operating for the Forces of Good).

⋀ Everyday Super Tip

In negotiation (and parenting, for that matter), do not make a threat you aren't ready, willing, and able to carry out.

Bill Eddy, attorney, therapist, and the world's leading expert on managing disputes involving people with high-conflict personalities, offers some advice on negotiating with bullies, which I summarize here, along with my own and that of other behaviorists:

Try building rapport. Flip the narrative. Don't assume that building rapport is a lost cause. A bully isn't expecting kindness or empathy in response to their high-conflict tactics. Employing empathy, listening, and rapport-building can be disarming. Channel your inner Nelson Mandela, who modeled the ultimate in empathy and compassion by actually befriending his oppressor. As he wrote in his 1995 memoir *Long Walk to Freedom*:

> I knew as well as I knew anything that the oppressor must be liberated just as surely as the oppressed. A man who takes away another man's freedom is a prisoner of hatred, he is locked behind the bars of prejudice and narrow mindedness.

Ignore them. You may think you can't ignore a bully because they are so confrontational. Try it. A behaviorist will tell you that ignoring undesirable behaviors is the most effective way to extinguish them. Like a windup toy, they might simply run out of momentum. In episode 10 of the *Forces of Good: The Superpower of Everyday Negotiation* podcast, my cohost Nina Greeley provides an example of a negotiation where she successfully employed this technique with a high-conflict negotiation opponent who aggressively persisted in criticizing her and the legitimacy of her client's case; she ignored the unprofessional and unproductive attacks until he had run out of steam. She refused to provide the resistance required for him to continue to push.

Avoid giving in. Bullies don't negotiate; they make demands, they threaten, they fight. High-conflict people are at war with the world around them and they go from relationship to relationship with intent to dominate. It's not always obvious. Some bullies are readily apparent and observable by a wide audience; others employ split personalities where the bullying behavior is carried out covertly when no one else can corroborate it; some bluster and put their prowess on display; others are cool customers appearing to be on the surface—ironically—ultra rational. With any flavor of bully, when they "win" by dominating, they still aren't satisfied. So they think they want more, and the cycle continues. Giving in to a bully doesn't bring relief because you have no assurance that the same thing won't happen in the future—and it does. Rinse and repeat. See the "Ignore them" strategy above. If negating undesirable behaviors is the most effective method to exorcise them, yielding to despotism only enables them.

Know your bottom line. This harkens back to the planning chapter. Before entering into a negotiation, know how far you're willing to go. If a team of people is involved, make sure you are all on the same page. Always know your BATNA (see Fisher & Ury and chapter 3) and when it's time to stop negotiating. You have to be firm about this.

Appear calm and patient. Bullies—also known as "high-conflict people"—love to get you emotional. Many are highly emotional themselves, though I've met several who are utterly cold and calculated, thus enjoying a heightened sense of superiority and power when they succeed in arousing your emotions. Try to stay calm and focused on what you want—even if you are just acting calm. High emotion and conflict is their playground and they are comfortable there. If you play into their home field advantage by trading something of substance triggered by raw emotion, they've already beat you. Instead, prepare yourself to be patient—very patient. The best negotiators aren't in a rush. Bullies generally are. Give the impression you have all the time in the world. If you appear desperate to settle, they will manipulate you into concessions you really don't want to make and may regret later, just because you want to get it over with. Instead, settle in for the long view.

Bring in a neutral decision-maker or mediator. If the attempts at negotiating drag on too long, suggest an outside decision-maker or mediator. In families, it's often a mutually agreed upon influential person in the family. If it's a neighbor dispute, propose going to a community mediation center, where people are trained to help. Often bullies don't like this idea because then they aren't the most powerful person in the room. It's hard for them to argue with the neutral person because that person won't be intimidated or influenced by their tactics. In the case of a neutral mediator or arbitrator, rules will apply. Like the reckless and arbitrary King of Hearts in *Alice in Wonderland*, who might torment you, might pardon you from a beheading depending upon his whim, or might simply throw a tantrum—and he was the more moderate ruler in Wonderland—bullies don't want to follow rules that are not of their own invention. The longer they can operate without third parties getting involved, the better chances that they'll retain their power and keep you guessing ("Will Troy take my milk money today or will I get a pass?" The chronic uncertainty perpetuated my fear and Troy's power which, like Wonderland's king, was rooted in his own fear).

Earlier I mentioned a bullying experience in 2021. I had been pointedly recruited to assume the role of president and CEO—succeeding a line of ninety-four years of men in that position—of a nearly century-old, predominantly white, cisgender male institution (and industry). My initial instinct was that it wasn't a good fit, and I said so (in addition to the conservative attitudes of the organization's demographic, past presidents generally had a background in finance or business. I do not. I didn't think I was qualified). In the end, I was wooed into accepting the position and emphatically assured that I was "just the right person at just the right time." Ever that wide-eyed, small-town girl from Illinois, I was naive and ambitious enough to answer a siren song beckoning a new era of women in leadership—to believe that the role represented a unique opportunity to introduce more diversity, equity, and inclusion into the organization now that I was a rarely invited female "insider." I was also the only attorney on the board of directors, and here's the plot twist that played out in the group bullying story arc successfully mobilized against me: The more I held my ground and stood up to them—rapport building and ignoring their barbs having failed through my many efforts to listen, encourage problem identification, and understand their perspective—*the more I may have been perceived as a bully myself.* I was disrupting the status quo, and ultimately realized I did not belong (see chapter 11). I understand now that I was an intruder—that my initial instinct had been correct. In fact, I wonder whether it's just possible I was chosen *because* I lacked a background in business or finance—to be a compliant "good girl" who would do as she was told by those who knew "better"—all the while displaying my picture on the wall and implying how "woke" they were to install a woman at the helm. "Just the right person at just the right time" indeed. I admit, I'm not too sophisticated to be conned. I'm also very trusting.

Remember the office manager from chapter 9 who had plotted ahead of time to put me, the "high-powered attorney," in my place? She had already stereotyped me as litigious because of generalized notions that attorneys are fighters. As the only attorney on this board of directors—and the one at the top of the pecking order —I believe the same song repeated, just on a different playlist. With my irksome DE&I agenda, I was received as a threat (brain's negativity bias, perceiving the stick for a snake—see chapter 11). Pile onto that the perception that attorneys "fight," and I was actually the "bad guy" in their narrative.

In the tamest of many examples I can safely share, I discovered that ballots, surveys and monthly invoices were sent only to the male account holders, not the women (account holders were assumed cisgender and dominantly heterosexual; I knew of just one same-sex joint account of the 1,150 account holders). Budgets, programs, committees, staffing, board directors, etc., were influenced—even decided—by ballots and surveys. Yet the women in the organization literally had no say, nor active notice of their financial liabilities (the legal incongruity of, effectively, ghosting one-half of the ownership on a joint asset was a separate conversation). "Oh Lucia," the chief operating officer—and echoed by a former board officer—attempted to placate me, "it's just that the practice is for those to be sent only to the primary email on the account. That's all." They may as well have said, "Nothing to see here. Move along." I did move along—digging deeper. I asked, "But *who* is the primary email on the accounts? I bet it's 95 percent men, and the 5 percent where it's the woman, they are mostly widows (who tended not to check their email). And it's not like we don't have emails for both joint account holders. We do. Scrape the data and report back to me." Sure enough—after multiple reminders—the data confirmed my estimation, give or take a few percentage points. The next so-called obstacle was: "But, Lucia, that's a software issue. The application assigns only one email address." (They may as well have said, "Nothing to be done. Software . . . out of our hands . . . what are you gonna do? Move along.") I did move along—inquiring with some IT experts and learned that reconfiguring the application to assign two emails was "easy as dirt" as one engineer put it. "Great! Let's make it happen," I decreed, "and while you're at it, add 'other / nonbinary' as an option to any surveys or applications that ask gender identity."

This issue of ballots, surveys, and invoices is but one of manifold unquestioned and long-standing practices and behaviors I called out in the organization, which contributed to an inequitable environment thrumming for evolution. Displeased with how I was upsetting the apple cart, leadership on both the operations and governance sides of the business made sure I knew—made sure I *felt*—the problems, delays, and extra work I was causing. Nine months into my term— which included my close inspection and overhaul of antiquated bylaws, nonexistent committee protocol and accountability, and vexatious board communication and management—I continued to bird-dog this issue (which still had gone unaddressed). The COO— the one who pulled the levers and turned the knobs to make things happen, the very one who so ardently had drafted me in the first place, and one who I had deeply trusted—progressively distanced himself from me. I wasn't behaving as the good girl he had recruited and expected. I bluntly shared with him the perspective that his (and others') complacency equated to complicity with the ongoing cam- paign of intimidation and bullying. He took umbrage. Exasperated, he finally seethed at me, "*I am not an agent of change!*" After that outburst, on a blustery Northern California wildfire-alert Tuesday in September, he barely spoke to me again.

The additional examples (and pattern of punitive scrutiny over women's products and services in particular), the extent of oppo- sition to my efforts, and the instances of disproportionately retaliatory conduct directed against me are too numerous and wretched to share within the scope of these pages. The messag- ing was unambiguous: "Lucia, you brought all this nastiness upon yourself. We warned you to quit pushing. You didn't listen. Only you are to blame." Suffice to say, I was the bully from their point of view—or at least a modern-day Cassandra (chapter 13). Despite deploying every gadget in my superpower utility belt, I was reluc- tantly drawn further into a fight by prolonged, highly organized, and legally suspect passive-aggression, aggressive-aggression, and ego-driven motives at seemingly every turn. Remember Axelrod's four tit-for-tat rules to maximize cooperation and outcomes from chapter 2? I was holding out on the fifth rule he espoused:

◢ Everyday Super Tip

Axelrod's fifth rule (see chapter 2): once the other party has defected from cooperation three times, so do you—permanently. They have proved themselves untrustworthy and either unwilling or incapable of playing nice; you need to either prepare for war or walk away.

In the meantime, dozens of women in the organization were imploring me in person and in writing, "You can't back down, Lucia. We're counting on you!" Even my sixteen-year-old son, who had a front-row seat to this reality theater, commented: "Mom, you can't let these guys beat you up like this. Your problem is that you're a Jedi. You need to be a Sith." (For the uninitiated, this is a *Star Wars* reference.) He wasn't wrong (recall, again, Axelrod's tit-for-tat rules and that one of my co-dominant TKI modes is Competing—chapter 12), but the context was also one of community with relationships at stake (Richard Shell—chapter 3). Sure, I'm trained to fight (figuratively from my "boot camp" years in litigation, and literally from years of martial arts and boxing training), but combat is poison for my soul (see chapter 9). I felt stuck.

Author and philosopher Peter Sage calls the dynamic that I believe unfolded in 2021 the Law of Conformity. If you hang out with nine motivated, go-getting, positive individuals, you're going to become the tenth. If you hang out with nine recreational drug users, you're going to become the tenth. The only other outcome is that you leave the group. Environment will trump intentions just about every time.

⋀ Everyday Super Tip

You don't change an environment; an environment changes you. Your two choices are to (1) conform to the environment or (2) leave. Feel like you can't walk away from a negotiation? Feel like you're stuck? You may not be as "stuck" as you think. Revisit your BATNA. Consult an objective confidant.

The year 2021, the same year in which this bullying situation descended steadily into Dante's Ninth Circle of Hell, was a treacherous year for human behavior. Polarization on a national level was fractal within local communities. The politicization of the COVID vaccine and mask mandates, cancel culture, a movement to mistrust the voting system, all opinions represented as incontrovertible fact . . . we witnessed amygdala hijack (see chapter 11) and galvanization at a national level that played out in our own backyards. My situation turned out to be highly politicized and so deeply rooted in sexism and bullying that I never stood a chance. I was that slightly exhausting superwoman with too much ambition flying in male-dominated airspace. I was a "type." Yet I remained unflaggingly optimistic—probably too much so and for too long (see overconfidence effect, chapter 13)—that my training in the behavioral sciences and experience as a mediator could rehabilitate a toxic situation and reshape behaviors.

"This is productive disruption," I reassured myself. "I need to hang in there and just get to the other side of it." So I tried harder. But in trying harder and in being drawn unwillingly into a fight, I failed to notice that the Law of Conformity was casting its spell. *The more I stood up to them, the more entrenched I became with them because I was operating in an environment where bullying wasn't just tolerated, it was promoted.* By the time I realized this dynamic, it was too late. My heart had been crushed and my reputation (and relationships) tarnished in the process. In my persistence to make "progress," I failed to read the room. I was like a determined ant marching purposefully north on a mission of equity, diversity, and inclusiveness, unaware that each footfall tread on the back of an elephant heading south. I wish I could offer a denouement more triumphant than the fact that surveys and invoices (not sure about ballots) were, by year's end, distributed to all account holders. Was that "progress"? If so, it was exacted at a tyrannical price. Another likely outcome is that, as an individual embodying principles of diversity, equity and inclusion, those principles were delegitimized by dethroning me.

⋎ Everyday Super Tip

If you're looking for magic potions, revisit your favorite J.K. Rowling title. These negotiation tools aren't foolproof, and superpowers aren't impervious to setbacks. Reflect and learn from obstacles. Measure success not by avoiding defeat but by recovering from the inevitable blows along the way and fine-tuning your skills and interoception (chapter 4).

The deepest daggers weren't lodged by the bullies themselves, but by my many so-called allies, who watched, who had knowledge, and who remained mute—their silence implicitly aiding and abetting the mistreatment—and the demoralizing feeling that I had let people down by ultimately deciding to walk away. I checked in with my son, concerned about what lessons he was internalizing from the situation. "You didn't let anyone down, Mom," he reassured me. "You have a heart in a game where the heartless win."

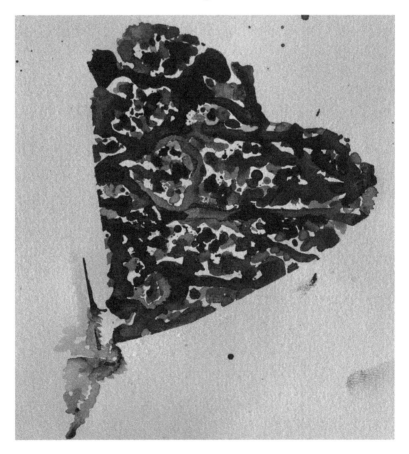

S. Lucia Kanter St. Amour, *Heartless Game*. Watercolor on paper.

As I reflect on the various bullying experiences in my own life (as well as in the lives of those for whom I've advocated and mediated), I now wonder if social proof (see chapter 13) may be an effective path—and not by just one person but a posse of peers. The group of bullies in 2021 triumphed because they outnumbered me. My allies vaporized, owing to at least two overpowering currents: (1) They couldn't risk their own place in the male tribe; and (2) they feared the bully-in-chief orchestrating the group. The bully, to be vanquished, must be eclipsed. These days, with assorted social media apps at the fingertips of adults and youth alike, we can collectively "cancel" a bully at speed and scale: that is, condemn them in a flurry of social media posts that results in the bully's social estrangement. This is a thorny approach. As cautioned by Barack Obama, the youth trend to "cancel" peers for not being 100 percent politically "woke" 100 percent of the time is judgment—not social justice or progress. As he aptly put it, "The world is messy; there are ambiguities."

What I might advise my kid self growing up in the pre-personal computer, social media, or smartphone era is to combine a **no-oriented question** (see chapter 10) with organizing a coalition of peers (**social proof**) to confront Troy, my childhood bully. That is, starting with close friends and expanding out, ask, "If I got ten of us together to all tell Troy to knock it off, would it be unimaginable for you to be one of those ten?" And once I got a "no" (meaning yes!) response from them, we would gather and make a plan for the moment of reckoning.

Once those Silicon Valley tech geniuses down the road from me invent a safe and reliable time machine, I'll give that a try and provide a full report.

CHAPTER 16

THE MARKETPLACE OF IDEAS: WHEN THE FIRST AMENDMENT CRASHES YOUR NEGOTIATION

Free speech! It's a constitutional and cultural hallmark of the United States and other countries as a protector of dissent and non-conformity. When is the last time you visited the "marketplace of ideas"—or it was visited upon you? If you drink at all from the firehose of social media, the visitations are hourly and numerous.

The "marketplace of ideas" concept of freedom of expression has been around since the English philosopher John Stuart Mill coined the term in 1859. It is based on the same theory of economics that superior products sell better than inferior products: thus, spurious speech will be filtered out while the worthiest ideas rise to the top. It was Justice Oliver Wendell Holmes who, in a 1919 Supreme Court case, introduced the "marketplace" idea into judicial analysis, and since then it has been repeated by the Supreme Court to oppose censorship and support freedom of thought and expression. It is a powerful idea.

Suffice to say, technology and society have evolved since Mill and Justice Holmes so purely preached that the free competition of ideas is the best way to separate falsehood from fact. Is it still relevant? Was it ever a reliable theory? And what does this have to do with everyday negotiation and your life?

In recent years, "fake news" has become a pervading paradox to dismiss facts that are disliked over personal opinion—which then is tweeted and followed and elevated to a point of eclipsing objective fact. Certainly, some falsehoods are a product of misinformation unwittingly posted by regular folks and spread through the blogosphere. But it has also become a business model. Entrepreneurs seek to generate revenue by contriving "information"—false or vapid acting as no obstacle to posting—to garner advertising; to create "clickbait" and "content" designed to circulate solely for the purpose of circulating but with no "there" there. The idea of a "Big Lie" is hardly new, and a remarkably effective mind control strategy to get entire populations to do what you want. Increasingly disconcerting is the predominant paradigm of opinions equating to facts with the art of dialectical discourse fading like a watermark on the Bill of Rights, and disrupting our personal lives, negotiations, and conflict scenarios.

Has the "marketplace" of ideas crashed, with free speech running amok? Could it simply not withstand the relentless demagoguery of social media, which Mill and Holmes could never have imagined? Founding Father James Madison believed that the First Amendment was the triumph of reason and humanity over error and oppression. But reason only carries humanity so far, and Mr. Madison never signed up for Instagram.

Astrophysicist Neil deGrasse Tyson teaches that there are three categories of truths: objective truth, personal truth, and political truth. He warns against asserting a truth before making sure it's not just an opinion you desperately want to be true. Propaganda is ancient. But I have to ask: if a post by the boy crying wolf surpasses one million views, does the wolf evolve from fiction to fact?

And now a challenge to Dr. Tyson: is there such a thing as objective truth? And what happens when the marketplace of ideas crashes in our own backyard, threatening our job, family status, business venture, or peaceful relationship with a neighbor?

> ## ⟋ Everyday Super Tip
>
> As a mediator, my long-standing refrain is that there are not two sides to a story. *There are actually two different stories.*

For each party their story is real, valid, and factual. In my 2021 bullying story from chapter 15, I am the fallen heroine and other characters constitute the group bully. Consider that they are the heroes of their story—the champions of "traditional values" who delivered upon me the punishment I deserved.

Philosophers throughout the ages have grappled with the question of objective fact, with varying perspectives. Plato is known for a distinctive view of objective reality. He asserted roughly that the greatest reality was not in the ordinary physical objects we perceive around us but in what he called Forms, or Ideas (see "Plato's Tree," chapter 14). And then there was Friedrich Nietzsche . . . (anyone?): His Twitter followers might scroll posts that exhort how we humans are constantly in developmental transition, but never arrived. While Nietzsche did not plainly reject truth and objectivity, he did reject the notions of absolute truth, external facts, and non-perspectival objectivity. In other words, no one has access to an absolute view of the world cut off from perspective; instead, all such *viewing* occurs from some particular point of view which in turn influences how things are perceived.

For individuals navigating our own stories, as well as for a mediator observing, listening, and learning the stories (and attitudes about "facts") of parties breaking through conflict or trying to make deals based on "information," it is useful to bear in mind that we are not fully in control of our own story. We are interwoven with one another, forming and being reformed as we move through the world. As the moral philosopher Alasdair MacIntyre has offered, our actions are constantly woven into the webs of others. Embracing this realization can neutralize some of the insidious loneliness and arrogance of the singular perspective (fueled also by confirmation bias; see chapter 13) of our subjective narrative. But it requires curiosity—or at least some unfulfilled need to move forward (e.g., "If I can't negotiate the cost of COBRA coverage and a positive reference, I risk future job opportunities and replenishing my child's medication, which is essential to the well-being of my family").

The fact that one is engaged in conflict—and the untangling of it—through mediation or negotiation at all, while uncomfortable for many people, is very promising because conflict is a signal that something is ripe for change. Leveraging this opportunity for change in the best light possible for the characters of your story may mean releasing your grip on the "facts" as you understand them. To let in something new, you may need to let go of something else.

⚡ Everyday Super Tip

The best advice I can offer when absorbed in a negotiation with another party whose casual abandon of facts cannot be transformed by reason and data is to *not place too much importance on those facts*.

WHAT?

Yes, an attorney trained in analytical reasoning and evidence (and absorbing the insights shared by Mari Fitzduff; see chapter 11) just advised you to **not place too much importance on facts in a negotiation**.

Negotiation in the dealmaking category probably should be based on as much empirical evidence as possible, in contemplation of how things could fall apart down the road and in consideration of contingencies. The more you can preempt conflict from the outset before the different stories diverge in the future, the better chance you have of avoiding the conflict resolution category of negotiation at a later date. If you do find yourself in that place, bear in mind that peacemaking strategies based solely on rationality and logic are limited. Also recognize that memory is faulty (including yours); we use numerous heuristics (see chapter 13) to make sense of the world and survive every day, including editing and adjusting past events to fit the current situation. Find out what emotionally matters to the other side and how your stories are interwoven and informing one another. *Ask what you each might lose if you don't reach a deal.*

During my teaching years, I assigned my students a role-play exercise called "Land Sale," which was part of the Center for Negotiation and

Dispute Resolution curriculum at UC College of the Law, San Francisco. I assigned confidential facts to the owner of a piece of land, whose deceased father had built a home there and was described by the son/current owner as a "big man" about town, and separate confidential facts to the real estate developer seeking to purchase the land. The parties on the opposing sides of that simulated negotiation were equipped with facts that never really had a chance of aligning. The problem was designed to make a deal *seem* impossible. In the course of the ten years I assigned "Land Sale" to students, maybe 10 percent of them figured out the "secret" to getting an agreement with the landowner (which, as it turned out, they could purchase for just $1): the heart of the problem lay in the landowner's memory of his father. What mattered most to him was that his father be memorialized. While the problem was written with enough hints to be dropped by the landowner during the course of conversing with the real estate developer, the student playing the latter role needed to employ keen listening skills (the simulation was ordered in the curriculum after the Listening module) and had to abandon reliance on empirical data to discover the "key" to cracking the case. They needed to set aside their facts and data and say, "Tell me more about your father" (see also the power of storytelling, chapter 8). Otherwise, it was as if the two parties weren't even speaking the same language.

The "marketplace" of ideas may be in crisis as people cling to their own "facts" on a spectrum of objective supportability. But like our own individual (or organizational) conflict, I choose to believe the disruption is not only productive but necessary for progress—which takes time, is not neat and linear, and happens in increments. When you find yourself mired in mess with sets of divergent facts that can't share a pizza together, try another approach altogether. You are a player in a process that could be ripe for a major breakthrough.

CHAPTER 17

THE PAUSE HEARD ROUND THE WORLD: NEGOTIATING YOUR INNER VOICE

Were you watching? Did you see it?

In March of 2022, Americans watched the Senate confirmation hearings for President Biden's Supreme Court nominee, Judge Ketanji Brown Jackson. It was on day two . . . the several-second-long pause and sigh issued by Judge Jackson when a certain senator, referring to a children's book (with huge posters as a visual aid) that aims to teach young people about racism, asked Jackson whether she believes "babies are racist."

We don't know exactly what Judge Jackson was thinking in that moment. Many on Twitter and various news feeds opined about the centuries of social injustice borne by women, Black people, and Black *women*; the indignities they have endured in the professional environment; and the blatant and insidious prejudices and ignorance that persist today. To many, that sigh represented a suppressed scream as she summoned all her dignity and the strength of muted masses that had come before her—a showing of fortitude through restraint to achieve the long-range goal, like the forward-thinking student in the first class of the semester and the chocolate negotiations (the one who had leverage and didn't use it in that moment).

Although we don't know what was going through her mind in those few seconds, she may have quickly weighed the value of her inner voice, her conscience that said to speak up, stand up to what many described as bullying, publicly denounce the theatrics . . . or to quiet that voice . . . and decide to play the long game to become the next Supreme Court justice—the first Black woman to do so.

What does this have to do with you harnessing the superpower of everyday negotiation?

How many times have you negotiated with that inner voice? How many historical figures have we studied who took that risk, or who declined to do so because the social opprobrium was too great, the harm too damaging to their status, their families, their safety?

Social justice journalist and sociologist Eyal Press wrote a very important book on this very topic called *Beautiful Souls*. It's about ordinary people who defy authority and the status quo because that inner voice, that conscience, will not be quieted. What Press's book reveals is that these resisters, these bold dissidents who challenge convention, are not the radicals who solicit impassioned responses from the public. They are everyday people, so fierce in their convictions that they cling to their principles even when faced with an authoritative—even punishing—moral dilemma.

For example, a police captain on the Swiss border with Austria in 1938 refuses to enforce a law barring Jewish refugees from entering his country. In the Balkans half a century later, a Serb from the war-blasted city of Vukovar defies his orders to save the lives of Croats. At the apex of the Second Intifada, a member of Israel's most elite military unit refuses a command to serve in the occupied territories. *Beautiful Souls* culminates with the story of a financial industry whistleblower who loses her job after refusing to sell a harmful product she rightly suspects is being misleadingly advertised.

Now think about the #MeToo movement in the United States. Many #MeToo cases are not clear-cut. We have all heard stories of overreach and backlash. The way in which it unfolded was far from perfect—possibly focusing too much on toppling big names rather than pushing for systemic change—but undeniably powerful because of numbers: the sheer numbers of women who stepped up and named names. Individually, they could be called crazy. But not so much as a group. Unlike Judge Jackson taking her several seconds to weigh thoughts we may never know, many women weighed the risks in their minds for years, wrestling with the fallout from saying something versus remaining silent and suffering, trying to recover, wondering if they maybe *were* crazy, trying to get on with life and put the experience behind them. Many found vindication, relief in this movement. But then there are cases like that of Cissi Wallin, the Swedish journalist who did the same in a country that is touted as the feminist capital of the world. She waited a full eleven years before outing the high-profile male journalist who she claimed drugged and raped her. And when she did, despite the thousands of #MeToo stories tweeted to her, despite at least a dozen other women who came forth with similar narratives about that same man, she was sued and convicted for defamation for speaking up. It was 2017 when she tweeted the name publicly, and she continues to battle her legal case in 2022 in Sweden. The legal trajectory of Wallin's case has become *de rigueur* in other countries, including the United States: to speak up means to invite shame, humiliation, and a counterclaim for defamation.

Psychologists James A. Dungan, Liane Young, and Adam Waytz have studied the moral concerns in predicting whistleblowing decisions and reactions to those decisions. Is calling out the misdeeds of others an act of heroism or betrayal? As with the #MeToo movement, many were vehemently divided on this question when computer intelligence consultant Edward Snowden leaked highly classified information from the National Security Agency in 2013. Dungan, Young, and Waytz's research revealed a tension between two basic moral values: loyalty and justice/fairness. These moral foundations are often in conflict with each other, and we are faced with negotiating between them. Fairness and loyalty are both basic moral values, but some people prioritize one over the other. The research showed that people who valued fairness more than loyalty expressed greater willingness to blow the whistle (they would view Snowden as a hero) whereas people who valued loyalty more than fairness were more hesitant (they would view Snowden as a traitor).

Whether it's a matter of seconds or a matter of years, I'm guessing you can remember experiences in your life when you have had that inner negotiation with yourself and with two competing moral values. To speak up or to remain quiet—to favor a higher sense of justice or prioritize loyalty to the group or the status quo. If you do speak up, how do you do so? When? To whom? What will be the consequences? You might wonder: Could I lose my job? Friendships? Will my children become pariahs and emotionally scarred? Could I expose myself to liability, legal fees, years of additional turmoil? And for what? Will my voice make a difference? Will it help make progress? *Will it matter?*

I offer no magic formula. Whether its assisting Jews fleeing Nazis, healing the wound from bullying or harassment, pursing one's lips in the face of petulant questioning in a public forum for a high public office, or anything in between—how that balance is achieved in the clumsy quandary of social progress, morality, individual interest, reticence, and bravery is delicate and not one-size-fits-all.

⚡ Everyday Super Tip

Remember Paul Ekman and the refractory state (chapter 11), which lasts about twenty minutes? If possible, wait to react until the refractory state has passed. Go ahead and type out the uncensored message you'd like to say during the heightened state of emotion, and save it for later review, reflection, and/or consult with a trusted confidant. Once you hit "send," you can't take it back.

These inner negotiations can take from seconds to a lifetime. I don't expect them to end anytime soon. My everyday negotiation advice is to wait for the refractory state to pass, consult wise people you trust, journal your feeling and options (during and post-refractory state), weigh the benefits versus potential risks, and consider how you might manage the fallout and what allies and/or advocates you can marshal to back you up. Ask them specifically because you cannot assume the allies you think have your back truly do. I don't mean quiet allies—I could count inoperative allies by the handfuls throughout my 2021 misadventure—I mean active, out loud allies. Sometimes you do need to stick your neck out for the Greater Good, something so much more immense than one individual or insular group. In my opinion, that effort does matter. I've done it many times, and I have to believe that. Why? As I say in every episode of my podcast:

WE ARE ALL CONNECTED. We don't all get a national stage. What we do get is our own little corner of the world, and that is where we make a difference. All of those incremental actions and differences add up.

S. Lucia Kanter St. Amour, *Inner Voice*. Multimedia diorama exhibited at The DeYoung Museum, San Francisco, 2008.

CHAPTER 18

SPECIAL NEGOTIATIONS: EVERY DAY FOR SOME

While this topic addresses a category of negotiation not applicable to everyone, it does apply to many—every day. It's the superpower of raising a special needs child and negotiating an annual IEP (individualized education plan) with a public school pursuant to the Individuals with Disabilities in Education Act (IDEA). This is the federal law that requires public schools to deliver a "free appropriate public education" (FAPE) in the "least restrictive environment" to qualified students with eligible special needs by means of a plan crafted specifically for that student.

When my older son, Julian, was fifteen months, his pediatrician identified him as markedly developmentally delayed. We began several therapies three months later, and he was officially diagnosed with autism when he turned two. He still hadn't developed language and wasn't yet walking. We started using sign language with him, but he also had congenital hypotonia—born with low muscle tone and sensation—and had difficulty coordinating movements to even sign. So, we combined the signing with PECS

(Picture Exchange Communication System), which had me printing, laminating, and Velcro-ing hundreds of one-inch pictures of everyday objects (ball, apple, juice, park, car) so that my son could hand me a pictorial icon to represent a request.

In December of 2006, he was one month from turning three years old, which represented his transition from county regional center services to the school district. He had a team of interventionists, eventually totaling fourteen, that I was managing, and I had to prepare for his very first IEP meeting (the negotiation with the school district to determine educational placement and services, which is then memorialized in a technical and difficult-to-understand document, also called the IEP). I was also traveling back and forth each week between San Francisco and the UC Davis MIND Institute to participate in a research study with Julian that required me to track and log on a daily basis each gesture, sound, word, and phrase he used, to rate each on a five-point scale, and to engage in a specific play protocol for forty-five minutes each day, which needed to be recorded in video format and had its own daily log sheet. In the meantime, I had Julian's younger baby brother (Nathanael) attached to my hip, and I was teaching my negotiation class at UC College of the Law, San Francisco.

So what did I do? I marched myself through the same planning memo that I assigned my students (the one I described in chapter 3). While I'm tempted to share that memo here, its length and detail would add another fifty pages and cause your eyes to glaze over. So, I will simply summarize a few of the highlights.

I thought about which category of negotiation this was. It clearly qualified for the **hybrid transactional/relationship** category.

The **stakes** seemed asymmetrical: high for me but "just another student and IEP" for the district.

I developed the standards and norms I would use. I first turned to his current team and asked them for advice and progress reports. I then researched national and local standards and norms to use for the service level and types we intended to request from the district.

I **gathered information from the community and built rapport.** I made connections with people (teachers, other families, speech and occupational therapists, and psychologists who knew someone in the district in their field, etc.) to learn about past practice in what the district had provided (and refused to provide) to other students. Though IEPs are confidential, there are other ways to get information (once again, I emphasize the importance of developing rapport).

I conducted a **distributive versus integrative bargaining analysis** (chapter 1—chocolates): How could I "expand the pie" to challenge the status quo and past practice and push for unprecedented services? For example, neurological music therapy, though not a mainstream intervention, had been highly recommended, was supported by science, and we had started sessions already at our own expense. We had been told that the district had never subsidized neurological music therapy as a modality. Well, "never" is a long time, and unprecedented is not the same as impossible! So in the IEP meeting, I first secured their agreement that they had heard about the efficacy of early music therapy for autism intervention and the research supporting it. Then, after their initial (and predictable) *social proof* response—"We don't do that; we don't know of any district that provides neurological music therapy"—response, I continued:

ME: "I get that. Imagine [mediator language] being the first trailblazing district to do so [using a third party as an audience—other school districts, the community, their reputation]. **What would it take to make that happen?**"

They tried to flip my appeal to them as a potential pioneer with a practical obstacle:

ADMINISTRATOR: "We can't set a precedent that we can't repeat" [subtext, i.e., listening to what's not being said—and is not permitted by law to be said in an IEP—that it would be much too expensive if word got out that parents could ask for individual music therapy].

ME [gentle reminder that each IEP is *individualized* under the law]: "I can appreciate your concern about repeatability. What would happen if [more mediator language] the therapist came to the school site for "push-in" music therapy to the entire classroom [as opposed to a "pull-out" service where the student is pulled out of the classroom for individualized or small group services in a separate area]? That way every student in the class, including Julian, would benefit."

Guess what? The district funded neurological music therapy under those conditions. We got what we needed for Julian, and the district got to be a shining example of cutting-edge intervention while still saving face and being able to say that they can't authorize individual neurological music therapy. Better yet, the service would help every student in that class, not just one.

✔ Everyday Super Tip

"We don't do that / we've never done it before / there's no precedent for that" doesn't have to be a standard that you accept. Is there a way for you to challenge the status quo with a creative and practical proposal that provides expansive benefits?

By the way, the neurological music therapy "win" is an example of a "Pareto frontier," named for Italian sociologist and economist Vilfredo Pareto (basically, it's the idea of optimizing available resources to provide maximum opportunities and outcomes).

I anticipated the positions, arguments, and norms the district would use. For example, I suspected that, at some point, they would reference one or more of our demands and remind us that the district isn't required to provide the "best" program for a student; it is required to provide just an "appropriate" program. So, I was very careful with my G. Richard Shell "high, specific, justifiable" goals to demonstrate that what I was requesting wasn't the "best." It was merely "appropriate" and eminently reasonable. I even went so far as to mock up a separate itemized program in another document that represented what the "best" program for Julian would look like and to contrast it with our ask and concretely point out how we weren't asking for the "best."

✔ Special Super Tip

Avoid using the word "best" in an IEP meeting when requesting services. Use the word "appropriate."

I explored available resources to develop BATNA, WATNA, and MLATNA. I asked for a list of the school sites in the district with CDCs (Child Development Centers—this is where special education students start at age three until they enter kindergarten) and asked what the protocol was for visiting those sites. Again, I asked around about which programs were favored and disfavored by the parent and teacher community (social proof but verified by my own research). I identified the school placement we intended to request for our son according to its location, staffing, and autism pedagogy, which, naturally, was at the most highly sought after school in the district (scarcity effect!), where they had only one opening (double scarcity effect!)—and made sure to tour all eleven other sites—including interviewing teachers, paraprofessionals, principals, and parents, and preparing a six-page report after each visit—to articulate with specificity why each of those would not be an appropriate placement. I did, however, go into each tour with an open attitude that I might find one that was suitable (and was relieved to find a solid backup option). This time and labor-intensive step also helped me craft BATNA and WATNA.

I researched **the players** to the negotiation: First, I made sure the right people would be there (a) from the district who had authority to make a deal without some hidden "we'll have to check with our supervisor" car sales tactic being used on us; and (b) to support our position, use the right jargon, and understand technical and procedural points that were unfamiliar to us [asking for help]. Then, I researched who specifically from the district would attend the IEP meeting and learned any information I could about them to (a) build rapport and (b) conduct reconnaissance on their negotiating tactics (I learned some interesting little nuggets).

I prepared a **concession plan** (including decoy concessions). I did not expect the district to agree to our initial "high" bundle of asks. I left plenty of wiggle room while also being able to justify every request with objective data from multiple sources (and other experts sitting in the room to vouch for the data).

I offered a **proposed agenda and goals** in advance for their review, along with sending the district team, well ahead of time, my son's progress reports and assessments from current interventions with the intent of (a) starting the **information exchange** process in advance so that they couldn't use delay tactics (something many parents and teachers warned me about as a go-to ploy they routinely used); and (b) saving time and getting a running start. The advance memo I sent the administrator who would head up the initial IEP team, unlike that naive young attorney with the Longshore Union, definitely communicated, "Bring your A-game":

Dear [District Administrator and known District IEP Team Members]:

First, we wish to thank you for your efforts thus far in helping us schedule school site visits and agreeing upon an IEP date. [Focus on them and expressing gratitude] This is an important time of transition for Julian and our family, and we recognize that this is the beginning of what we hope will be a long and productive relationship. You'll find that we, as Julian's parents, intend to offer a great deal of positive contribution toward Julian's education and to support the people who work with him through ongoing communication and collaboration. [Robert Axelrod: start by being cooperating]

We ask that anyone who is necessary to participate in the IEP be available for the duration of that afternoon, as we both are. [communicating expectations] Our work schedules are rather unforgiving, and we suspect with the district's caseload, that time is equally precious for you [expressing empathy and shared interests]. Toward the common goal of making the most of the December 7 meeting, we attach the following categories of materials [information exchange, anchoring (a type of mental map and trap), and communicating expectation for them to make us a substantial first offer—i.e., "Don't try to lowball us with the same prepackaged deal I've heard from five other families."]:

1. November 2006 progress reports from Julian's current therapies;
2. Draft Goals and Objectives; and
3. Proposal for Placement and Related Services [make it easy for them]

We have put a great deal of consideration into these materials, and their contents are based upon a number of relevant sources including [authoritative and objective standards and norms]: applicable law; the ICDL [Interdisciplinary Council on Developmental and Learning Disorders] Guidelines; current MIND Institute research; the National Research Council Guidelines; past and current practice of [District] with other students on the autism spectrum; and the advice and counsel of experts in the law regarding IDEA, as well as a number of individual developmental pediatricians, psychologists, and other experts specializing in autism spectrum, including those who have worked with Julian over the past fifteen months [Authority principle].

We are also very eager to hear your ideas, as you have been doing this longer than we have [shows curiosity, openness, exploring interests, appealing to their "authority"] and anticipate that, working cooperatively with deference to appropriate practices and guidelines and discussing Julian's individualized needs [leveraging specific language from applicable law], we can make Julian's transition from Early Start to [District] a smooth one. This will also serve as notice that we intend to record the IEP [don't even think about trying the shenanigans that we've heard about. It will all be on record].

Thanks and we'll see you on the 7th.

Now, I couldn't research and plan for everything. We were just one side of the negotiation. So, I filled out a **Give/Get/Guard chart** and prepared a list of **questions.**

Importantly, I **reflected personally** on how I might be triggered during the process and how I could increase my effectiveness. I was scared. I perceived an **asymmetry in power** in that the school district held most of the cards; they were Mission Control, and no placement or related services would happen without their green light to set it in motion. I thought about how I could influence that perceived power and which **mode** to use (concluding that my natural TKI mode was suitable). While I recognized my **leverage** in that there could be no final agreement without my consent on every single point (and I was prepared to take as much time as we needed), how could I *feel* more powerful when I actually felt so vulnerable?

I turned to another cherished professional mentor, Barbara Chvany. Barbara was—and still is—a badass. She was a pioneer in the world of labor arbitration in San Francisco back when women in labor arbitration were unheard of (also back when women were not allowed to wear pants in the courtroom, mind you. Had to wear a skirt!). Nobody messed with Barbara, and I needed a piece of her with me in that IEP room. I had always admired a particular gold knot necklace of hers that she had acquired on a trip to Greece. Barbara loaned me the gold knot, and I walked into that IEP, sat at the head of the table, and **imagined** myself (chapter 6) as the most powerful person in the room.

I was patient. I kept them at the negotiating table over the course of four months and four separate meetings before signing a final document (though we prioritized agreement on his school placement early on and got him installed at the very school site we'd hope for while we continued negotiating related services). Not only was this a critical time in Julian's life when his brain was still elastic and he could realize the most gains from an aggressive intervention that could make the biggest difference in his life path; this was the foundational IEP upon which every subsequent annual IEP would be reviewed. I suspected that, each year, services and

⟋ Everyday Super Tip

You don't need to sign the IEP right away. Have the school/ district email you a draft. Take time to review it carefully, and think about whether it contains everything your child needs. Also, you can agree to part of the IEP and disagree with other aspects. That way, you can get programs going in the areas where you have agreement, while you continue to negotiate the other points. *Do not be pressured or rushed!*

resources would be chipped away. I was right about that, and each year I wanted to be able to "give" a little in the way of concessions where appropriate.

My dogged preparation for Julian's foundational IEP was absolutely critical, not just for obtaining concrete services but for managing myself during the process. Equally critical (and also made possible by the powers of fastidious preparation) was my presence of mind and **interoception** during the IEP negotiation sessions, and especially my keen **listening.** I recall a moment during the third meeting when the administrator (the one largely in charge, the one who clearly intimidated the teachers, psychologist, occupational therapist, speech therapist, and behaviorist) announced that "a decision has been made that Julian's physical therapy services will take place at a separate district site after school [far from the school and our home], with transportation provided." I was confused. No decisions are made without the entire IEP team, and we were never consulted. Had the team conferred in our absence? What did she mean "a decision was made"? When? By whom?

So I asked, "Who made that decision?" The administrator repeated, "A decision was made." Well, now my "Spidey senses" were prickling. She was using the passive voice and dodging my question. In the Robert Axelrod lexicon of chapter 2, she was **defecting from cooperation.** Thus, I retaliated immediately and proportionately in accordance with the tit-for-tat protocol—by publicly "canceling" her maneuver. One by one around the room I addressed each of the nine IEP team members individually, starting with the physical therapist:

"Did you make that decision?"

PHYSICAL THERAPIST: "No. I would provide services at the school site. I didn't decide that."

To the speech therapist: "Did you make that decision?"

SPEECH THERAPIST: "Me? No! I'm a speech pathologist. I wouldn't make that call."

To the psychologist: "Did you make that decision?"

PSYCHOLOGIST: "I did not, nor would I be the person to make such a determination."

I continued until I had exhausted everyone at the table. Then I reverted to the administrator and said, "Well, the entire IEP team is here, and it seems that no one made that decision. So I'm having a hard time understanding how 'a decision was made' on that point. Am I missing something?"

Unlike my experiences with bullies, I'm pleased to report a happy outcome to this story in that we enjoyed fifteen years of a collaborative and productive relationship with the many members of Julian's various IEP teams over the course of his public school education.

Julian turned eighteen in 2022. He did develop language and is the most persistent asker of questions I've ever met. He is also a determined and relentless negotiator! I now realize that the public school system and IEPs were the easy parts. Now he is an adult, and we are in a new phase of navigating programs, paperwork, and social rules and relationships in the "real world": the ABLE Act (a state-run savings program for eligible individuals with disabilities), Social Security, a conservatorship proceeding and order, a special needs trust, an adult transition program, future housing, a supervised job program. . . . And so it will continue. The negotiating and advocacy (*not* fighting) never ends, and not just with entities and agencies but with him as a human being who wants badly to be a "regular guy," to be independent but due to the severity of his condition, always needs supervision, oversight, and limitations placed on him.

At some point in the future that I'd rather not think too much about at the moment (but sometimes need to), Nathanael will be the one who helps Julian and may need to negotiate on his behalf. In fact, I sometimes think Nathanael is already Julian's greatest advocate and protector, not I. Siblings have the longest relationship of anyone with their brother or sister with special needs—a relationship that might span sixty-five-plus years. They are watching and learning (not to mention often becoming marginalized because a special needs sibling can loom larger than life in the family unit). To this day, when one of us adults in the family reaches what I would call **impasse** with Julian on any particular point (even just getting him to physically move from spot A to spot B), Nathanael is the one who breaks the impasse.

I remember a particular trip to Mariposa Grove in Yosemite National Park. It is the largest grove of giant sequoias in the park, with several hundred mature examples of the tree. Two of its trees are among the thirty largest giant sequoias in the world. Julian loves to be outside. Loves to hike, loves windy days, loves the snow. It was winter when we visited, cold, and getting dark, and we needed to get going. Julian didn't want to leave. He planted himself right on a tree stump and wouldn't budge. I tried to get him to move. My husband tried to get him to move. It was getting darker, I was cold, I was tired, we had a long drive ahead of us, I was now irritated . . . and Nathanael said to me, "Mom. Stay here. I got this." I watched Julian's younger brother trudge over to him as the glimmer of late afternoon sun on the snow receded with each footfall. I couldn't hear what they were each saying, but he talked quietly to him for about three minutes. Then I watched Julian rise from the stump and calmly walk back toward us with his brother.

I never did find out what words passed between them. It was a private negotiation between two brothers.

Eliza Ruffle, *Bionic Future Super-Me*. Original avatar.

ACKNOWLEDGMENTS

I had a running start in life growing up in a safe area with great public schools, in a family with two parents, and not worrying about basic needs being met. Such a stable foundation is not to be taken for granted and has allowed me to dare and love greatly. I wouldn't have accomplished half of what I've realized in life, not to mention weathered many struggles (notwithstanding my advantages), without the help of loved ones, friends, colleagues, and mentors.

Foremost, my cherished husband and soul mate, Frank, aka Frankie, aka Francesco. He "gets" me. He knows that he has to let me fly, even when he predicts (usually accurately) my wings are soaring perilously close to the sun and might melt; he knows he will be there to help pick me up and dust me off if I've over-estimated my reach, and without ever saying, "I told you so." This book came pouring out of me in 2022 as if my whole life had led up to it. During the fevered creative process, he rolled over many nights in bed to find me missing or was met with a terse (but loving) "I'm writing!" response when alerting me dinner was ready (a dinner he had cooked, even after working all day himself) and then placed the plate of food down next to me and planted a quick kiss on my bowed head. We should all be so lucky to find a partner in life who knows, loves, understands, and supports us like my Francesco. In addition to his boundless love for me, he became stepfather to two little boys, ages three and four (one with severe special needs), to be another father to them—as well as putting up with undefinable quantities of dog hair and dog slobber over the years. He has enriched all of our lives beyond measure.

Peter Kanter deserves special recognition. Thank you for being an excellent, dependable, stand-up business partner in the enterprise of raising our boys and for becoming my friend again after some years of distance between the two of us. You have been a wonderful example to our sons, and I'm glad to have you in my life.

To the two other main men in my life, my dad (Steve) and my brother (Mark): I talk to you both at length every week, and you have shown a consistent and deep interest in my life, my work, my feelings, my exploits. You have listened to me *ad nauseam* through my laughter and tears, through triumph and turmoil. You have been my ALLIES. When I lamented, through sobs, how I had "not been enough" to counter the bullies, you said, "You were enough. You are enough."

To my mother (Sunny), who was a working mom during the second wave of the feminist movement, in a small town in the Midwest where most of the other moms didn't work outside the home (and who shunned her for "neglecting" her latchkey children to pursue a career): thank you for giving me and Mark the gifts of freedom, trust, responsibility, and independence throughout our childhood and for being my role model—for setting the bar high enough that I wouldn't trip over it but reasonable enough that the struggle would be purposeful.

To my mentors: Chris Knowlton, Barbara Chvany, Ilia Salomone-Smith, Ken Silbert. You took me under your tutelage while I was still a college kid and stuck with me no matter what— continuing to this day. You lighted the way, coached me when I stumbled, toasted my milestones, and championed me (though without pumping false sunshine up my skirt). I wouldn't have gone to law school in the first place without your guidance and inspiration, wouldn't have started my own nonprofit organization where I saw a need and a void, wouldn't have summoned the strength to charge through some dark phases of my life and career. I am delighted to carry forward that mentorship myself with the next generations.

To my bright law students at two vibrant law schools over the course of ten years: You may have thought I was teaching you, but you fell for my con because the act of teaching made me a more refined negotiator, and you also taught me a thing or two. It has been a pleasure to witness your development as professionals, parents, and human beings.

The road to publication is paved with dangling modifiers, ambiguous antecedents, and tedious typesetting. Thank you to my editorial and production team—Eric Hübler, Ellen Tarlin, and Asya Blue—for whom no detail was too small to nitpick (and please don't start with me as to whether to capitalize after a colon: "Sometimes you do and sometimes you don't"). You saw the potential of this book in its draft form and said "This is real. Count me in." Any errors caught by readers are entirely on me, as one who continued to tinker—which is a no-no. In my defense, you can't leave a writer alone unsupervised with her manuscript for a month in between final proofreading and design!

SOURCES

Abrams v. United States, 250 U.S. 616 (1919).

Ariely, Dan. *Predictably Irrational: The Hidden Forces That Shape Our Decisions*. New York: HarperCollins, 2009.

Axelrod, Robert. *The Evolution of Cooperation*. Cambridge, Mass.: Basic Books, 2006.

Babcock, Linda, and Sara Laschever. *Women Don't Ask: Negotiation and the Gender Divide*. Princeton, N.J.: Princeton University Press, 2003.

Bennett, Craig M., Abigail A. Baird, Michael B. Miller, and George L. Wolford. "Neural Correlates of Interspecies Perspective Taking in the Post-Mortem Atlantic Salmon: An Argument for Multiple Comparisons Correction." https://www.psychology.mcmaster.ca/bennett/psy710/readings/BennettDeadSalmon.pdf.

Bordone, Robert. "How Do I Negotiate When the Other Side Has More Power? Negotiation 101 with Bob Bordone." https://www.youtube.com/watch?v=tHQTHXGiD_k.

Brown, Margaret Wise. *Goodnight Moon*. New York: HarperTrophy, 2007.

Cabinet Office Behavioural Insights Team. *Applying Behavioural Insights to Charitable Giving*. https://assets.publishing.service.

gov.uk/government/uploads/system/uploads/attachment_data/file/203286/BIT_Charitable_Giving_Paper.pdf.

Carter, Alexandra. *Ask for More: 10 Questions to Negotiate Anything*. New York: Simon & Schuster, 2020.

Center on the Legal Profession, Harvard Law School. "Separating the People from the Problem: Colin Rule and the Rise of Online Dispute Resolution." *Remote Courts* 6, no. 5 (July/August, 2020). https://thepractice.law.harvard.edu/article/separating-the-people-from-the-problem/.

Chance, Zoe. *Influence Is Your Superpower: The Science of Winning Hearts, Sparking Change, and Making Good Things Happen*. New York: Random House, 2022.

Cialdini, Robert. *Influence: The Psychology of Persuasion*. New York: Harper Business, 2006.

Covey, Stephen R. *The 7 Habits of Highly Effective People: 30th Anniversary Edition*. New York: Simon & Schuster, 2020.

Dungan, James A., Liane Young, and Adam Waytz. "The Power of Moral Concerns in Predicting Whistleblowing Decisions." *Journal of Experimental Social Psychology* 85 (November 2019), article 103848. https://doi.org/10.1016/j.jesp.2019.103848.

Eddy, Bill. *5 Types of People Who Can Ruin Your Life: Identifying and Dealing with Narcissists, Sociopaths, and Other High-Conflict Personalities*. New York: TarcherPerigree, 2018.

Eddy, Bill. *BIFF: Quick Responses to High-Conflict People, Their Hostile Emails, Personal Attacks and Social Media Meltdowns*. Scottsdale, Ariz.: HCI Press, 2011.

Ekman, Paul. *Emotions Revealed: Recognizing Faces and Feelings to Improve Communication and Emotional Life* (revised edition). New York: Owl Books, 2003.

Ekman, Paul. *Telling Lies: Clues to Deceit in the Marketplace, Politics, and Marriage.* New York: W. W. Norton, 2009.

Fisher, Roger, and William Ury. *Getting to Yes: Negotiating Agreement Without Giving In.* New York: Penguin Books, 2011.

Fitzduff, Mari. *Our Brains at War: The Neuroscience of Conflict and Peacebuilding.* New York: Oxford University Press, 2021.

Gino, Francesca. *Rebel Talent: Why It Pays to Break the Rules at Work and in Life.* New York: Dey St., 2018.

Harari, Yuval. *Sapiens: A Brief History of Humankind.* New York: Harper, 2015.

Holmes, Anna. "The Radical Woman Behind 'Goodnight Moon,'" *The New Yorker,* January 31, 2022. https://www.newyorker.com/magazine/2022/02/07/the-radical-woman-behind-goodnight-moon.

Kahneman, Daniel, and Amos Tversky. "Prospect Theory: An Analysis of Decision Under Risk." *Econometrica* 47, no. 2 (March 1979): 263–292. http://www.jstor.org/stable/1914185?origin=JSTOR-pdf.

MacIntyre, Alasdair. *After Virtue: A Study in Moral Theory, Third Edition.* Notre Dame, Indiana: University of Notre Dame Press, 2007.

Mandela, Nelson. *Long Walk to Freedom: The Autobiography of Nelson Mandela.* Time Warner Books UK, 1995.

Mill, John Stuart. *On Liberty* (Project Gutenberg edition). https://www.gutenberg.org/ebooks/34901.

Medvec, Victoria H. *Negotiate without Fear: Strategies and Tools to Maximize Your Outcomes.* Hoboken, N.J.: John Wiley & Sons, 2021.

Murphy, Annie Paul. *The Extended Mind: The Power of Thinking outside the Brain.* Boston: Houghton Mifflin Harcourt, 2021.

Nietzsche, F. *Beyond Good and Evil*. Chichester, U.K.: John Wiley & Sons, 2020.

Norton, Michael I., Daniel Mochon, and Dan Ariely. "The IKEA Effect: When Labor Leads to Love." *Journal of Consumer Psychology* 22, no. 3 (July 2012), 453–460. https://doi.org/10.1016/j.jcps.2011.08.002.

Plato. *The Republic* (514d–519d).

Pogue, David. "The Worst Advice You've Ever Received (and Are Willing to Pass On)," *New York Times*, April 30, 2019. https://www.nytimes.com/2019/04/30/smarter-living/best-advice-youve-ever-received.html.

Press, Eyal. *Beautiful Souls: Saying No, Breaking Ranks, and Heeding the Voice of Conscience in Dark Times*. New York: Farrar, Straus and Giroux, 2012.

Rueb, Emily S., and Derrick Bryson Taylor. "Obama on Call-Out Culture: 'That's Not Activism,'" *New York Times*, October 31, 2019 (updated August 10, 2020). https://www.nytimes.com/2019/10/31/us/politics/obama-woke-cancel-culture.html.

Sage, Peter. "How to Eliminate Self Doubt & the Power of Your Unconscious Mind." TedXPatras, December 2019. https://www.ted.com/talks/peter_sage_how_to_eliminate_self_doubt_forever_the_power_of_your_unconscious_mind.

Shapiro, Daniel. Negotiating the Nonnegotiable: *How to Resolve Your Most Emotionally Charged Conflicts*. New York: Penguin Books, Reprint edition, 2017

Shell, G. Richard. *Bargaining for Advantage: Negotiating Strategies for Reasonable People*. New York: Penguin Books, 2006.

Shulman, Michael. "Alan Alda Is Still Awesome," *The New Yorker*, June 12, 2022. https://www.newyorker.com/culture/the-new-yorker-interview/alan-alda-is-still-awesome

Strohmet, David B., Bruce Rind, Reed Fisher, and Michael Lynn. "Sweetening the Till: The Use of Candy to Increase Restaurant Tipping." *Journal of Applied Social Psychology* 32, no. 2 (February 2002): 300–309. https://doi.org/10.1111/j.1559-1816.2002. tb00216.x.

Tannen, Deborah. "Gender and Family Interaction." Chap. 8 in *The Handbook of Language and Gender*. Hoboken, N.J.: Blackwell Publishing, 2003.

"Transcript: Ezra Klein Interviews Annie Murphy Paul," *New York Times*, July 20, 2021. https://www.nytimes.com/2021/07/20/ podcasts/transcript-ezra-klein-interviews-annie-murphy-paul. html.

Ury, William. *Getting Past No: Negotiating in Difficult Situations*. New York: Bantam Books, 1993.

Vedantam, Shankar. "You Don't Need a Crystal Ball." *Hidden Brain*, March 28, 2022. https://hiddenbrain.org/podcast/ you-dont-need-a-crystal-ball/.

Voss, Chris, with Tahl Raz. *Never Split the Difference: Negotiating as if Your Life Depended on It*. New York: HarperCollins, 2016.

Ward, Wendy, *Charm Book*. St. Petersburg, Florida: Montgomery Ward & Co., 1964

ABOUT THE AUTHOR

S. Lucia Kanter St. Amour has been practicing law since 1998. Ten years of her practice included regular clinical teaching positions in mediation and in negotiation and settlement at both University of California law schools at Berkeley and San Francisco. She has lectured at many prominent law and business schools in the United States and Europe and served for a number of years as an annual competition judge and mediator for the International Chamber of Commerce in Paris. One of the designers of the pilot mediation program for the Equal Employment Opportunity Commission's San Francisco regional office in 1996, Lucia has a deep background in mediation and earned her mediation certification from the Harvard Law School Program on Negotiation. In 2022, she launched her podcast, *Forces of Good: The Superpower of Everyday Negotiation*, and was elected vice president of the board of directors for the flagship San Francisco chapter of United Nations Women. She is the mother of five boys (three canine and two human) and founder and executive director of Spectrum Strategies, a 501(c)(3) nonprofit organization providing siblings support, and dog matching and training to families of children with autism. Studied in six languages, a pianist, a golfer, and a home cook of really legitimate Italian cuisine, she lives with her family in the San Francisco Bay Area.